CONTEMPORARY NATIONALISMS:
Persistence in Case Studies

By
Louis L. Snyder
Professor Emeritus of History
The City University of New York

AN ANVIL ORIGINAL

Under the general editorship of
Louis L. Snyder

D1482469

KRIEGER PUBLISHING COMPANY
Malabar, Florida

1992

Original Edition 1992

Printed and Published by
KRIEGER PUBLISHING COMPANY
KRIEGER DRIVE
MALABAR, FLORIDA 32950

Library of Congress Cataloging-in-Publication Data

Snyder, Louis Leo, 1907–
    Contemporary nationalisms : Persistence in case studies / Louis L.
Snyder.
        p.   cm.
        "An Anvil original."
        Includes bibliographical references and index.
        ISBN 0-89464-570-6
        1. Nationalism   2. Nationalism—Case studies.   I. Title.
    JC311.S547   1992
    320.5'4--dc20   91-14474
                                                                                  CIP

10   9   8   7   6   5   4   3   2

TO
JOAN AND DON SACAROB
WITH RESPECT, DEVOTION, AND LOVE

In the production and publication of this Anvil, I have been most fortunate in having the able assistance of my better two-thirds, Ida Mae Brown Snyder. She has been more collaborator than keen-eyed editor. Every author knows the pitfalls of the publication process, from the incorrect date to the unnecessary cliché to the careless split infinitive.

CONTENTS

Part I
Nationalism in Current Society

PART I

NATIONALISM IN CURRENT SOCIETY

CHAPTER 1

INTRODUCTION

CONTROVERSY. For centuries there has existed among peoples everywhere a consciousness of belonging together. In the late eighteenth century this state of mind developed into a powerful ideology that has continually grown in importance. It first engaged the attention of Europeans and then spread to all corners of the world. In an effort to understand this vital historical force, scholars and observers differ in their explanations of its many facets. There is some ground for these differences. Nationalism is beset by many inconsistencies, contradictions, and paradoxes. What seems clear to one analyst can be hopelessly confusing to another.

An example is that of national character, a concept closely related to nationalism. National character has been defined as the totality of tradition, interests, and ideals which are so widespread and influential in a nation that they mold its image in the minds of the country's people. But does national character exist? On the one side, there is Henry Morley's view that in the literature of any people we perceive under all contrasts of form produced by varied social influences "the one national character from first to last." As early as 1753, David Hume, Scottish philosopher, historian, and innovator of modern metaphysical thinking, stated that where a number of men are united into one political body and use the same speech or language, they contract a resemblance in their manners and have a common or national character, as well as a personal one peculiar to each individual. This idea was repeated in 1927 by British scholar Ernest Barker. He saw each nation, starting from the raw stuff of its material basis, building up a sum of acquired tendencies. Then it settles into the unity and permanence of form which we call national character. (*See Reading No. 1.*)

By no means has this favorable estimate of national character attracted the acquiescence of all scholars of nationalism. Thus, British scholar Hamilton Fyfe denounced Ernest Barker's view and called the very idea of national character an illusion. In

Fyfe's view, because no nation can show a consistent line of action, none has a national character. The idea, he wrote, has been uncritically accepted as fact, though actually it is as much a fiction as the supposed flatness of the earth. (*See Reading No. 2.*)

These differing views on the idea of national character present only one of the controversies on the subject of nationalism. Not the least of the problems associated with nationalism is the question of whether this historical force is now in decline and in the process of being succeeded by some new loyalty such as a world state. Or is it now as vital as ever and even stronger in its present phase? Here again there are advocates on both sides. It is the theme of this study that nationalism is not in decline but instead has shown an extraordinary staying power as it persists in the minds of human beings. Nationalism in the twentieth century has been an outspoken and realistic historical force. If anything, it has become more widespread and powerful at the end of the century than at its beginning.

In the contemporary world virtually all the peoples of the more than 159 nation-states regard their sovereignty as sacrosanct and inviolable and recognize no diminution of their independence. They hew first and foremost to their national heritage and revere their flag and anthem. All pledge in their own way to be dedicated to peace, but it is not altogether certain that they have completely abandoned the state of mind that can lead to war. The nationalistic urge is to stay with traditions and a special way of life. Power politics still operate, both openly and covertly, in international relations. Patriotism and national pride come first.

WEAKENING OF NATIONALISM? Those who see a weakening of nationalism in the contemporary world and a process of dismantling national systems present varied arguments for their view: (1) Increased cross-cultural interaction is lessening the nationalistic we/they image of other peoples in the world. (2) The *intermestic* (merging of *inter*national and do*mestic* issues) nature of politics is creating a heightened sense of internationalism. (3) The nation-state can no longer cope with problems such as ecology, food production, and disease prevention. (4) In a supersonic nuclear age, the state can no longer protect its people. (5) Given its history of causing conflict, nationalism is condemned by the moral judgment of history. (6) Multinational corporations and independence are ending economic nationalism. (7) There is an undefinable, but real psychological trend toward a new world order. International organization is expanding and transnational philosophies have a strong appeal. In these views, a diminution of nationalism is under way.

Much of the sentiment about the waning of nationalism is due to the disgust engendered by its evils and to the desire that it be ended in human affairs. Albert Einstein, great physicist and amateur political sage, rejected the philosophy of nationalism and opted for internationalism. He did not want to keep secret his international orientation. He said that the state to which he belonged did not play the least role in his political life. He saw it as like the relationship with a life insurance company. There were observers who agreed with the scientist who had escaped the monstrosity of Hitlerism. Their distaste for what they believed to be a scourge of mankind led them to predict its end.

Even important scholars of nationalism hold that it has had its day and is in decline. Hans J. Morgenthau, a prolific scholar, writer, and activist, was concerned with the subject of nationalism and contributed much to its study. He saw the national state as obsolescent and enmeshed in decay as a result of the technical and military conditions in the modern world. He believed that nationalism as a powerful political sentiment was being replaced by larger regional units which would be better attuned to the new conditions and might well call forth a more effective vehicle for competition between nations. (*See Reading No. 3.*)

Morgenthau admitted that nationalism would not necessarily be mitigated by a successful regionalism. "The nations of Western Europe, for instance, are too weak to make themselves singly the effective spearhead of nationalism. The time has passed when the French or Germans could dream of making the world over in their own image. But if the nations of Western Europe were able to form a new political and military unit of very considerable potentialities, they would then have acquired the power base for a new nationalism, common to all of Western Europe. Then they could compete effectively with the nationalism of the two superpowers. That the traditional nation-state reflects the technological and military conditions of the contemporary world is obvious. Yet its replacement by larger regional units, better attuned to these conditions, may well call forth a more effective vehicle for nationalist opposition."[1]

Another distinguished political scientist, Karl W. Deutsch, believes that blind nationalism, like totalitarianism, is obsolescent in our time, in either peace or war. He sees the whole thrust of the technological development as pushing beyond wars. In his view there will be a pluralistic world of limited international law, limited but growing. We are experiencing a qualitative and quantitative transformation of mankind in our own time. We can anticipate a change in our societies, first in the most advanced countries in the world, and then, in the long run, for all mankind. (*See Reading No. 4.*)

As political scientists, both Morgenthau and Deutsch saw no reason to avoid predictions for the future. On the other hand, historians in general tend to avoid prognostications about the future and limit themselves to discussions and analyses of the past. They see nationalism as a powerful and formidable historical movement in the contemporary world, but they decline to predict its future course because in their view anything might happen. British scholar E. J. Hobsbawm refuses to accept this notion and plunges wholeheartedly into a discussion of the future of nationalism. In his *Nations and Nationalism Since 1789* (1990), this Marxist historian turns his attention to a phenomenon as diverse and contradictory as nationalism; he does not like what he sees.

Hobsbawm judges that nationalism is no longer a major vehicle of historical development. This conclusion apparently is based on his own hostility to it as much as on the march of events. For him nationalism (as well as the nation itself) is an obnoxious nuisance, especially when it refers to national identification. He argues that urbanization and industrialization undermine the nationalist assumption of a territory inhabited essentially by an ethnically, culturally, and linguistically homogeneous population. He is so disgusted with the existence of nationalism that he remarks that no serious historian of nations and nationalism can be a committed political nationalist. In his

[1]Hans J. Morgenthau, *Truth and Power* (New York, 1970), p. 275.

view of Hobsbawm's book, Stanley Hoffmann of Harvard University judged that "Mr. Hobsbawm on nationalism is a bit like a deaf man writing about music." (*See Reading No. 5.*)

STAYING POWER OF NATIONALISM. Throughout his career Hans Kohn, pioneer in the study of nationalism, described it as one of the determining forces in modern history. From Europe, where it first appeared, it spread throughout the world. In Kohn's view, the continuing stress upon popular sovereignty and cultural distinctiveness hardly helped to promote cultural cooperation among peoples. Although he recognized that there were technical and economic reasons for making the peoples of the world more interdependent, Kohn saw nationalism as a persistent historical phenomenon, growing rapidly in importance everywhere. As a historian, Kohn devoted his many works to discussions of nationalism in the present era. He avoided any predictions or comments about its future. (*See Reading No. 6.*)

A similar point of view was presented by Boyd C. Shafer, who also refused to join the ranks of those who were certain on what would happen to nationalism in the future. "I am a historian," he writes. "I cannot predict." He asked a pertinent question: "If we are to have, at any future time a truly international order, above the nations, or if we are to have a world state, the international or world government would have to grow as national governments did, and if it is to have substance and viability, if indeed it is to exist, it will have to touch the vital interests of each world citizen. It, too, will have to grow, as nationalism did, out of the concrete fears and hopes, desires and actions of people who are passionately interested in its maintenance. It will have to afford the promise of a better life and, at the same time, protect man in the ways national governments have." Shafer said modestly that he just did not know whether this would happen. "Whether or not we have time in this age of national hydrogen bombs, I do not know." Shafer simply declined to put himself on record by predicting confidently on a way out of the "never-ending circle" of nationalism. (*See Reading No. 7.*)

Like historians, journalists also are concerned with the impact of nationalism on contemporary life. We can observe in their news stories and editorials a tremendous interest in how nationalism has affected the lives of people throughout the world. Headlines tell the story: "NATIONALISM AT ITS NASTIEST." "NATIONALISM UNCORKED." "YET MORE NATIONALISM." "RISING NATIONALISM THREATENS U.S. BASES." "THE SOVIET UNION IS COLLAPSING INTO A CLAMOR OF INDEPENDENT-MINDED REPUBLICS AND ETHNIC GROUPS." More and more, reporters and editorialists are turning their attention to a historical force of such extraordinary power. Most do not see nationalism as disappearing in the overwhelming wave of a united world. Instead, they judge nationalism as a most powerful and resilient force that just refuses to go away.

Indicative of the judgment of nationalism by journalists is the view of George Brock, foreign editor of *The Times* of London and commentator on current issues. He sees it as an ism that will not go away and as a historical force of the utmost importance. He deems it incorrect to look at the new Europe and conclude that nationalism is buried in it. He criticizes the intellectual fashion of new advocates of Pan-Europa to push nationalism back into the dustbin of history. Nationalism, he writes, has maintained its power during the past two centuries and, if anything, has increased its strength. He points to what is happening everywhere: emotions are running high all over the world as great crowds unfurl their flags and deck their recapture of pride and identity in the traditional national colors. This is not happening yesterday; one sees it displayed by emotional people everywhere in the world, from the smallest to the largest nations.

Journalist Brock reveals a sense of history when he sees the power of nationalism as more resilient than the outward form of the national state. He describes the rise of nationalism as a response to the changes in the modern industrial world. The old agrarian society, together with its religious faith, was succeeded by an educated, merchant, and industrial society, and the focus of political loyalty shifted. The idea of the nation received love and allegiance—and it still does. In Brock's view, the power of nationalism has constantly been underestimated. "Nationalism will survive."

A CLUE TO PERSISTENCY. What is behind the persistence of nationalism in an era of increasing international communication and transnational activities? Not the least important explanation is that human beings tend to cling to any historical movement that can give them a sense of security in a dangerous world. Many millions of lives were snuffed out in the tragic crucible of two World Wars. The loss in property values cannot even be estimated. In times of peace when the Great Powers live in comparative peace, there are always "minor" conflicts that take the lives of unfortunate peoples. The blood spilled is quickly forgotten.

People everywhere seem to be convinced that there is safety in security—"in union there is strength." They turn to the national flag and the national anthem for support against "those others." People who live in a contiguous territory and feel bound together by language and historical customs and traditions place enormous emphasis upon their right to self-determination. Hence, their strong support for the historical force generated by that sense of belonging.

Neither the League of Nations (generated in horror by the losses of World War I), nor the United Nations (calling for peace after the overwhelming blood bath of World War II), has been able to cast nationalism aside in favor of a global internationalism. Both have had difficulties in their roles as parliaments of mankind. The Soviet Union turned to dissolution as clamorous minorities called for satisfaction of their own national sovereignty. Mini-nationalisms asked for recognition of their own national identities as against the central nationalism which they saw as holding them as hostages. A viable internationalism seems remote as a goal for peoples caught in the foils of persistent nationalism.

Nationalism is, of course, a global phenomenon. It is the accepted way of political life for nation-states scattered throughout the world. It is behind the popular flag-anthem syndrome in our time. It is the dominating urge of the many dissatisfied regional nationalisms seeking freedom and independence. It is obvious that all these nationalisms cannot be treated at length in this small Anvil volume. But attention is given to outstanding case histories of either centralized or disintegrative nationalisms, or by both. These special case studies reveal a historical force still operating strongly in a troubled world.

In the treatment of contemporary nationalisms, greater attention is given here to the mini-nationalisms struggling against the centralized nationalisms. Much observation has been paid hither to the centralized nationalisms. In this volume the exploding mini-nationalisms or regional nationalisms calling for independence deserve greater attention.

CHAPTER 2

UNITED STATES OF EUROPE: REALITY OR EVANESCENT DREAM?

PROPOSAL FOR EUROPEAN UNITY. The advocates of European unity predict the gradual waning of nationalism in the contemporary world and the emergence of a continent in union—what they see as a United States of Europe. They accept the idea that countries that for centuries have been bitter enemies will forgive their adversaries and join together in mutual good will and prosperity. They believe that the European Community will at long last be transformed into what could be a European nation. In other words, they see contemporary Europe as working toward continent-wide monetary, financial, and economy policies. This is expected to lead to a "comprehensive stability" that will meet the challenge of social and environmental change. In this view the ongoing urge for economic unity will eventually lead to political union. It is claimed that declining nationalism will definitely be succeeded by a continent-wide unity.

Those who oppose the belief of the Eurocrats reject their views as fallacious. They contend that, although European nations are willing to join together for their mutual economic benefit, each one balks at the idea of diminishing or losing its national sovereignty. Representatives, they say, will pay lip service before the European Parliament, but have no intention whatsoever of sublimating their national identity. The buck stops with the raising of the national flag. The idea of transferring national power to a continental centralized parliament is abhorrent to national-minded administrators. To such critics the very idea of European political unity is simply impractical, unrealistic, unattainable.

THE LABORS OF COUDENHOVE-KALERGI. Behind the goal of a united Europe was the figure of a solitary idealist who devoted his life to continental unity. Proceeding under the assumption that a United States of Europe was not only a possibility but a certainty, he hewed to the line that nationalism was outmoded, not only dangerous but stupid. Despite obvious signs that national consciousness was not only prevalent but persistent all over the world, he insisted that it was dying as a powerful factor in human affairs and that a united Europe was well on the way. He put every effort into his cause and never deviated from his goal. (*See Reading No. 8.*)

It was a classic case of a one-man crusade. Richard M. Coudenhove-Kalergi (1894–1972), of Austrian background and later a research associate in history at New York University, became a zealous champion of Pan-Europa. From 1924 on, he produced a long series of books devoted to his goal. He called for the reorganization of the world into six autonomous units— the British Commonwealth, the Soviet Union, Pan-Europa, Pan-America, China, and Japan. He sought for the support of such distinguished statesmen as Walter Rathenau, Thomas Masaryk, Aristide Briand, and Winston Churchill. Did not Churchill in 1946 at a speech in Zürich say: "The peoples of Europe have only to wake up one morning and resolve to be happy and free by becoming one family of nations, banded together from the Atlantic to the Black Sea for mutual aid and protection. One spasm of resolve. One single gesture." All such statements encouraged Coudenhove-Kalergi to believe that he was on the right track. But the sponsor for a United States of Europe failed to see that this encouragement was given by leaders who themselves were infected with the creeping vine of national egoism. Without exception they declined to head the movement for Pan-Europa. As early as October 1926, Coudenhove-Kalergi headed a European Congress in Vienna, the first of what was to be a series of similar congresses. In 1947, at a meeting held in Gstaad, Switzerland, the European Parliamentary Union was established with Coudenhove-Kalergi as its Secretary-General.

The movement was growing slowly, but it lacked a mass base. Coudenhove-Kalergi tried desperately to keep it alive. He drafted a constitution for a United States of Europe. He saw the development of a European Parliament and believed implicitly that it would one day replace the parliaments of separate national states in Europe. He failed to understand the strong competition between national European parliaments and the European Parliament. At the root of the issue was the proper exercise of national sovereignty. Many European nationalists believed that any acquisition of legislative competence by the European Parliament would necessarily come at the expense of their own legislative bodies. They were certain that the European Parliament would inevitably seek to exercise powers it did not already possess. They argued that it was unrealistic to divest European states of their national sovereignty.

According to critics, Coudenhove-Kalergi failed to understand that European nations looked inwardly despite their agreement for economic unity. National independence, they insisted, was a basic fact in European life, and efforts to minimize it would not be successful. Coudenhove-Kalergi simply refused to accept that argument.

SCHUMAN, MONNET, AND THE EUROPEAN COMMON MARKET. Behind the creation of the European Economic Community was the dedicated work of two French statesmen. Both were convinced that the union of European states was vital not only for France but for the entire continent.

Robert Schuman, born in Luxembourg on June 29, 1886, was brought up in Lorraine, at that time a German province. In World War I he refused to serve in the German armed forces and spent the war years in a German prison. After the fall of France in 1940, he was arrested by the *Gestapo* and again imprisoned. Escaping in 1942, he worked with the Resistance until France was liberated. Then he devoted his energy to a brilliant political career, serving successively as Minister of Finance, Premier, Foreign Minister, and Minister of Justice.

A man of strong religious faith, Schuman believed that the salvation of Europe could be found in its original Christian roots. He would work for a new moral and spiritual climate in which a united Europe would flourish. He was convinced that the traditional enmity between France and Germany could be abolished through the creation of a European community based on the equality of each confederated state under a common authority and discipline. In his view, this would open up undreamed of perspectives. The continent had "a noble primacy"— a goal decreed by Providence. This was a continental necessity.

Europe must strengthen itself, not only in her own interest, but in the name of humanity. The good of Europe, he said, was identified with the welfare of mankind.

Linked closely with the ideas of Schuman was the work of Jean Monnet, political economist and diplomat. He was born at Cognac on November 9, 1888. From 1919 to 1923 he held the post of Deputy Secretary-General of the League of Nations. In World War II he worked for the Free French movement as Commissioner of Arms, Supplies, and Reconstruction. After the war he was responsible for drafting plans to rebuild French industry. Like Schuman, he believed that there could be no real peace in Europe until quarreling nation-states accepted the idea of continental unity. The countries, he said, were too cramped to ensure their people a prosperity that modern conditions made possible. Their continued development was impossible, he warned, unless they formed themselves into a common economic unit and a federation. In 1955 he organized the Action Committee for a United States of Europe and in 1956 became its president.

Both Schuman and Monnet supported a step-by-step process leading to a continental combination. They claimed that a fragmented Europe was responsible for the loss of millions of lives and untold damages to property. In their view, the time of the nation-state was ended. National sovereignty would fade into the textbooks of history.

In 1950, Schuman, while Foreign Minister, acting together with Monnet, introduced the Schuman Plan, which proposed to place the national coal and steel resources under a supranational authority. The project called for an eventual continent-wide unity. In 1952, the European Coal and Steel Community (E.C.S.C.), forerunner of the Common Market, was formed. Six nations (France, the Federal Republic of West Germany, the Netherlands, Belgium, Luxembourg, and Italy) pooled their coal and steel resources under a common supranational control. (*See Reading No. 9.*)

The preliminary work of Schuman and Monnet led eventually to the Treaty of Rome, signed on March 25, 1957. Thus was formed the European Economic Community (E.E.C.). The treaty contained not only the basis for a Common Market but also outlined in general additional policies intended to lead to a full economic union. (*See Reading No. 10.*)

THE EUROPEAN PARLIAMENT. Eurocrats were not satisfied with the progress thus made. For them this was merely the first step toward the goal of political integration. June 7, 1979, became for them a time of joyous fulfillment. On that day, some 179 million people of the European Community voted in an election for the European Parliament. For the first time there were common European elections. After decades of debate, the move had finally been made from economic to political unity.

From its very beginning the European Parliament had to face the excruciatingly difficult problem of relations with national parliaments. It soon became obvious that the individual parliaments had no intention of throttling even a part of their national sovereignty. A balance between national and supranational elements was never adequately achieved. There was transnational union on paper and in extensive debate, but it was not achieved in the European Parliament. There was no real legislative power in the new continent-wide Parliament. Critics judged it to be mired in political impotence.

NATIONALISM AS CHAMPION. Despite the enthusiastic claims of the Eurocrats, it was obvious that the European Parliament was merely a shadow body unable to break the grip of national sovereignty. Nationalism had triumphed in the struggle for control. What explanation can there be for the snail's pace toward the achievement of a United States of Europe?

First and foremost, there was no mass movement calling for the transfer of sovereignty from the national to the European level. The citizens of the nation-states of Europe continued to see their primary loyalty to their own countries. Eurocrat leaders failed to see that a mass acceptance was basic for so critical a move. Instead, they argued eloquently on an intellectual level among themselves, convincing each other of the necessity of their sacred cause, but failing to achieve mass support. A consensus of approval was lacking. Virtually all citizens of the European states continued to regard themselves as patriots in their own countries.

Despite the survival and progress of the Common Market, the nation-states looked increasingly inward. This view persisted even though there was increasing conformity in many aspects of European life. European nationalists hold rigidly to their belief that nationalism was the right way and that no continent-wide political unity expressed in a United States of Europe could solve rivalries between the nations. They accused Eurocrats of preaching an ineffective internationalism on a continent of sovereign national states. The issue remains unresolved.

THE CHANNEL TUNNEL. Enthusiastic Eurocrats point to the near completion of the English Channel Tunnel in late 1990 as a giant step in the coming of European unity and an end to the isolation of Great Britain.

Toward the close of the Ice Age some 10,000 years ago, a cataclysmic flood poured over a wide plain and thereby created the English Channel. That body of water acted as a great moat and shut off Britain for centuries from the rest of the continent. It acted as an effective deterrent to invasion. Neither Napoleon in the first decade-and-a-half in the early nineteenth century nor Adolf Hitler with his victory-minded legions in the mid-twentieth century dared to cross the English Channel with a frontal assault on the British.

The Channel Tunnel was truly a phenomenal project, a twenty-three mile shaft cut through a bed of solid gray-blue chalk. A British team drilled southeast from Dover, while a French unit pushed northwest from Sangatte. The tunnel borers worked behind huge drills weighing as much as 1,300 tons and using rotary blades up to twenty-eight feet across. There are three arteries—two for passenger trains, a third for maintenance crews. There is a network of 100 crossing alleys. After the opening in 1993, trains will speed through in twenty-six minutes. It is, indeed, a massive enterprise, the longest underwater passage in the world.

Yet, the claim of the Eurocrats that the Channel Tunnel will contribute to the lessening of British nationalism is not shared by many Britons, who see it as a challenge to their sense of "noble separateness." From their point of view it is fine to shorten the trip to France and thereby avoid the seasickness associated with the Channel, but they regard it as a far cry from the loss of national sovereignty. The sentiment of English patriotism was voiced as early as Shakespeare: "This blessed plot, this earth, this realm, this England." (*See Reading No. 11.*) The Eurocratic prediction that this mammoth project means a diminution of British nationalism is dismissed as unrealistic exaggeration.

CHARLES DE GAULLE AND FRENCH GLORY Strong opposition to the idea of European unity was voiced by two powerful leaders. It is reasonable to assume that Charles de Gaulle and Margaret Thatcher reflected the view of many of their people when they chose nationalism instead of political unity of Europe as their preference. After the defeat of France by Nazi Germany in 1940, de Gaulle assumed the leadership of Free France and bore the cross of Lorraine in the struggle against Hitler. He thought of himself not merely as the leader of his country, but he was France itself. His mind was like the Louvre, filled with pictures of battles in which the French were always victorious. France could not be France without greatness. (*See Reading No. 12.*)

De Gaulle's attitude toward the Common Market hardened when he became convinced that its Eurocratic leadership was working for a common European government. As President of France, he began to place barriers in the way of Common Market expansion. He attacked architects of the Common Market as "a technocratic, stateless, and irresponsible clique." He would not allow decisions affecting the superior interest of France to be imposed by a "stateless bureaucracy with its supranational pretensions." Eurocrats were appalled by his hard line. Jean Monnet, his countryman, was concerned: "The most striking thing about General de Gaulle is his nationalistic view of world affairs."

De Gaulle never wavered in his fear that European economic integration would lead to political unity. In his view, unity was impossible unless a European political union was organized, led, and controlled from Paris. After all, was not Paris not only the center of Europe, but also the fulcrum of the entire world? De Gaulle had no intention of relinquishing the tiniest element of French sovereignty to a political parliament representing Pan-Europe. He believed that the powers and duties of the

French executive belonged only to his government. He poured scorn on what he termed "the European hybrid." He presented a constant theme: European integration meant "vassalage and subordination to the United States." In placing his faith in the permanence of nation-states, de Gaulle delivered a powerful blow to the idea of European unity.

MARGARET THATCHER AND LITTLE ENGLAND NATIONALISM. After eleven and a half years as British Prime Minister, Margaret Thatcher on November 22, 1990, resigned her office. It had been a notable career. Her steady hand in control of Britain earned her the sobriquet of "The Iron Lady." Thatcher believed it to be desirable to make economic accords with other European countries as long as it helped the national pocketbook, but to extend economic union into political accord was anathema, an idiotic fallacy, an impossibility in the age of nation-states. She believed that the national interest was best served by holding to the idea of national sovereignty.

Thatcher's view was bolstered by her understanding of British history. For generations, if not for centuries, it has been a cardinal tenet of British foreign policy to stay out of the interminable European quarrels. It was a concept of "splendid isolation"—it was best for Britain to stay away from clashes on the Continent and to prevent any one nation from acquiring too much power. On two critical occasions in the twentieth century, when the aggressive nationalism of Kaiser Wilhelm II and Adolf Hitler followed an expansionist policy, Britain went to war to prevent what was seen as an impossible situation. But between these major wars there was a retreat into the traditional view that Britain must remain aloof and use its great natural moat—the English Channel—to protect itself against invasion from the Continent.

Thatcher held consistently to her belief that the projected United States of Europe was a faulty conception and that it would do more harm than good. In a speech delivered at the College of Europe in Brussels in September 1988, she spoke sarcastically about the notion of European federalism. She rejected any notion "of suppressing nationhood and concentrating power at the center of the European conglomerate." She expressed her opposition to a European super-state exerting a new dominance. On another occasion she said: "A man may climb Everest for himself, but at the summit he places his country's flag." Again and again she was attacked for her views on a united Europe, but she struck back with ridicule and scorn.

NATIONALISM REASSERTED. The judgment of Margaret Thatcher was simple and direct. "Creation of a federal Europe? Over my dead body!" European statesmen spoke enthusiastically about the virtues of an economic—and political—union of the nations of the Continent, but actually many agreed with the blunt statements of Britain's Iron Lady. Each European nation-state is the product of a desire for security. Peoples living in a contiguous territory, speaking a common language, and fortified with historical traditions sense that they belonged together and resent any effort to lessen their national identity. Their consciousness of "belonging" is a powerful factor in their lives. They regard this sentiment of togetherness as a sacred trust and they reject any efforts to diminish their sovereignty.

Eurocrats argue zealously about their cause. But the sentiment of nationalism is deeply engrained among peoples who are unwilling to risk their national identity in favor of a questionable future. Nationalism persists because the people of European national states want it.

THE GERMAN CONNECTION. The cause of the Eurocrats received a transfusion in late 1990 with the reunification of Germany. The German government at Bonn, including Chancellor Helmut Kohl, architect of German unification, Foreign Minister Hans-Dietrich Genscher, and Federal President Richard von Weizsäcker, all have warmly supported the idea of economic unification and favor the extension into political unity. They want to see the new Germany democratic, prosperous, and *culturally* nationalistic, but in united Europe. They see the two German states as the driving force behind a development that overcomes the division of Europe. They regard the European Community as a bedrock of stability for the whole of Europe, a source of hope for European nations. They believe that integration must be resolutely advanced, with a monetary and economic union supplemented by an intergovernmental conference for achieving major progress on constitutional matters. In their view, the new Germany must never be dominating or domineering. Above all, they reject the aggressive nationalism that in the past had resulted in terrible consequences for the German people and for the world.

Eurocrats have interpreted these views as sliding closer to political integration. Europe today, they say, is moving closer to the target of political union in this century. They admit that the progress of the European Community's past performance has been at a snail's pace and that national interests frequently prevail over Community interest. But now, they say, more power will be vested in the European Parliament, and a European citizenship will be introduced. They believe that German leaders have thus far avoided saying too much about political union, largely because they have been preoccupied with German unification. The new Germany, they insist, will turn eventually to political unification. They quote Thomas Mann, who in 1952 stated that Germans do not want a German Europe, but a European Germany.

The citizens of the new Germany reject the kind of aggression that has brought them such tragic results. They do not want a too powerful Germany to cause anxiety in other European states. For Eurocrats this is the kind of support they need to bring into existence the desired United States of Europe.

CALLS FOR EUROPEAN UNITY. Despite the persistence of nationalism and ethnonationalism throughout the Continent, the Eurocrats went ahead with their plans for the leap to unity. Led by Chancellor Helmut Kohl, who had pushed the drive for German reunification, the twelve leaders of the European Community met at Maastricht in a special session of the European Parliament and approved treaties that would forge common economic, foreign, and defense policies. The idea was to propel Europe into the 21st century as a cohesive power able to meet challenges from the United States and Japan. The most important economic decisions were to have a single currency, a single foreign policy, and a single code of laws by 1999. Kohl insisted that German experience with the evils of nationalism in the 20th century caused Germans to support a vital restructuring of Europe. "The way to European unity," he said, "is irreversible."

At Maastricht the British complained that European union would include numerous contentious political questions. They insisted that only the British Parliament could make a decision to abandon the once mighty British pound. British Prime Minister John Major accepted the plan with strict reservations about British sovereignty.

Whether the pact toward European unity will be successful by the end of the century remains to be seen. It will have to overcome the powerful consciousness of nationalism still existing in Europe.

CHAPTER 3

NATIONALITIES IN THE SOVIET UNION: THE BALTIC REPUBLICS

THE COMMUNIST EXPERIMENT. Working at his desk in the British Library, Karl Marx came to the conclusion that at last he had found what was wrong with mankind. In 1848, together with Friedrich Engels, he issued the Communist Manifesto. Accepting the materialistic conception of history, they wrote of an inescapable class struggle, the inevitable triumph of the proletariat, and the certain establishment of a Communist society. "The Communists openly declare that their ends can be attained only by the forcible overthrow of all existing social conditions. Let the ruling classes tremble at a Communistic revolution. The proletarians have nothing to lose but their chains. Workingmen of all countries, unite!"

That call to action was muted until the Communist Revolution of 1917, when the old system in Russia was overthrown, the Czar and his family executed, and the first great experiment in communism was introduced under the leadership of Lenin. On the death of Lenin, there began a struggle for power between Leon Trotsky, advocate of a permanent global revolution, and Joseph Stalin, who opted for Russian nationalism, building social revolution in one country first. The feud ended with the assassination of Trotsky. Stalin went on to direct the course of the first "Great Experiment" in communism. By 1934 he abandoned collective leadership, established his personal rule, and threw out or exterminated all personal and potential enemies. His harsh dictatorship was characterized by nationalism, xenophobia, and anti-Semitism. The "dictatorship of the proletariat" was transformed into the dictatorship of one man. All opposition was crushed in his favor.

For the next several decades after its successful war against Hitler, the Soviet Union, along with the United States, was regarded as a superpower. A cold war began between the two countries. Convinced that the capitalist world aimed to destroy the Soviet Union, Stalin appropriated enormous sums of money

everywhere. It rejected the cold war and mended relations with the United States. The Kremlin agreed to the reunification of Germany and looked on helplessly as satellites in Eastern Europe turned away from Soviet influence. Throughout the Soviet Union itself Communist Party officials were thrown out of office. There were even demands for democratic elections, an unheard of procedure for more than seven decades. The Communist society, as envisioned by Marx and Lenin, had proved to be a gigantic failure. The Great Experiment seemed to be collapsing in a fury of rejection.

THE NATIONALITIES PROBLEM. The Soviet Union was composed of a plethora of some 100 nationalities with scores of languages. This problem was not new; it had been an annoying burden in the nineteenth century for the Russian Empire. With Gorbachev's new *glasnost* and *perestroika* the citizens of the subject nationalities were emboldened for the first time to speak openly of their anger. They saw the Communist system as grotesquely inefficient, and they wanted a change in their status. Masses of demonstrators began to appear on the streets demanding that the distrusted Communist Party be thrown out of power. The new mood was an astonishing development. It was a call to action against the throttling hand of the Kremlin. In the Stalin era the dictator had allowed tens of thousands of kulaks (well-to-do farmers) to starve. He executed comrades, even Old Bolsheviks, or anyone, including innocents, whom he suspected of being dangerous for his personal power. His secret police flourished in what was supposed to be the society of the future. His country took on the characteristics of a slave state. His successors carried on in this ghastly tradition that power lay in the hands of the leader while the proletariat had to accept a rigid centralized control. This was supposed to be the "dictatorship of the proletariat" envisioned by Karl Marx.

Slowly but surely, movements of dissent began to appear in all the constituent "republics." Masses of people, at first hesitantly and then confidently, protested the iron grip of the Communist Party. For decades the Soviet people had endured misery and frustration as Party members confiscated the available necessities of life. While the people suffered, capitalist

Germany and Japan, smashed almost beyond recognition by the crushing defeat of World War II, recovered and went on to prosperity. A new revolution was in the making.

In effect, the problem was the result of two conflicting kinds of nationalism—the centralized nationalism of the Kremlin against the compounding calls by the regional nationalisms of the nationalities. With its economy in disarray and its nationalities clamoring for freedom from the center, the Soviet Union was in a serious crisis. In the past the secret police helped maintain the fiction that all was well. Fortified by propaganda, the ship of state sailed on with little understanding among the Party hierarchy that it was in danger of sinking.

SOVIETS SEIZE THE BALTIC REPUBLICS. The news left a trail of astonishment throughout the entire world. On August 23, 1939, Foreign Ministers Joachim von Ribbentrop and Vyacheslav Mikhailovich Molotov signed a nonaggression pact between Nazi Germany and the Soviet Union. It was agreed that the two countries would not go to war against each other for ten years. The news was incredible, sensational, and stupefying. The two dictators, Adolf Hitler and Joseph Stalin, had been sworn enemies. For years each had heaped abuse on each other. Hitler had excoriated Bolshevism as the arch enemy of civilization, and, in turn, Stalin denounced the Nazis as Fascist beasts. The pact was a surprising addition to the bitter war of words.

For Hitler the agreement was an unmixed boon. Now he was relieved of the fate of Kaiser Wilhelm II, who had been caught between two fronts in World War I. The Nazi leader would not forget the menace of Bolshevism—he would wait for the right moment and then smash it into oblivion. Stalin, too, saw immense advantages in the pact. For some time he had dreaded a combination of Britain, France, and Germany, capitalistic nations, directed against him. Moreover, the Soviet Union had been weakened by Stalin's military purges, and the dictator wanted time to prepare for defense. He needed all the time he could get to complete the military industrialization envisioned by the Third Five-Year Plan.

Added to the Hitler-Stalin nonaggression pact was a secret cynical protocol giving Stalin the right to annex the independent Baltic states. Hitler recognized that Latvia and Lithuania belonged to the Soviet sphere of influence. In the following September, after Poland was smashed and divided between the two dictators, Lithuania was annexed. The Kremlin then demanded that the three Baltic states should agree to permit the construction of Soviet military bases on their territory. The way was now open for Soviet Russia to take all the three states. On July 14–15, 1946, the Kremlin held rigged elections in the Baltic states in which only Moscow-supported candidates were listed. Lithuania, Latvia, and Estonia were overrun. Their national independence was rejected and Communist governments installed. The upper hierarchy, including politicians, military personnel, and high officials, vanished. Many were arrested, imprisoned, or executed. Authors, publishers, businessmen, the cream of Baltic society, were deported along with their families. The economies were integrated into that of the Soviet Union.

BALTIC REACTION. The Baltic peoples had never willingly accepted outside interference. They always had a sense of territory and the feel of history, essential ingredients of modern nationalism. Their belief in sovereign nationhood remained strong and they resented any attempts to thwart their belief in independence. In the past they rebelled against invaders. Russian rule was extended over the three states in the eighteenth century. In the late nineteenth century the Baltic peoples, encouraged by reforms in the Russian Empire, began to demand their freedom. In World War I German and Polish troops fought over control of the area. After 1918 the Baltic peoples were given their independence, a policy recognized by Moscow. All three peoples set up independent republican governments, which flourished until 1939. Western nations, including the United States, did not recognize the annexation of the Baltic states.

For more than four decades the Baltic peoples were restive under Soviet domination. The Kremlin proceeded with its policy of Russification, but Baltic national sentiment was never obliterated. The Baltic peoples held to their languages, traditions, and religious practices. They yearned for freedom from Kremlin control. They were aware that most of the constituent republics of the U.S.S.R. called for an end to Communist control. The idea of independence attracted more and more support.

The urge for freedom became more intense when the Baltic peoples learned how Stalin had won domination over their lives. On August 15, 1988, their suspicions were confirmed when for the first time they heard about the secret protocol in the agreement between Stalin and Hitler in 1939. Hope began to arise that the new spirit of openness would ease the way to freedom. Such hopes began to fade when the Soviets blandly denied the existence of any secret pact.

LITHUANIAN NATIONALISM. One of the fifteen republics of the U.S.S.R., Lithuania lay on the shores of the Baltic Sea. It was one of the westernmost areas of the Soviet Union. Relatively small in size, it has an area of 26,173 square miles, with a population (1988 est.) of 3,682,000. Its capital is at Vilnius. The country produces cattle, hogs, and electrical appliances. Despite its small size, it possesses an ancient culture. Its history was a story of subjugation by foreigners. Lithuania fell under the control of the Livonian Knights in the thirteenth century. Its people fashioned a sovereign state and controlled sections of neighboring territory. Christianity was introduced in the late fourteenth century and the country became strongly Catholic. It was merged with Poland in 1569. In the three successive partitions of Poland (1772, 1791, and 1799), Lithuania passed to Russian control. In February 1918 it became an independent kingdom under German protection. Occupied by the Russians in 1940, it was absorbed into the U.S.S.R.

During the policy of Russification, the Lithuanians continued to place great stress upon their country's traditions. The original heritage of Lithuanian folklore had been handed down from generation to generation. Lithuanian songs, fairy tales, and legends had their roots in a language and culture that were among the oldest in Europe. This inheritance and its contribution to Lithuanian nationalism persisted even during the days when the Russians extended their control. Moscow, aware of the resentment in Lithuania, attempted to mute national sentiment by rewriting Lithuanian history for its schools and promoting the cause of Soviet ideology in textbooks. Soviet annexation of the country was described as a glorious chapter in Lithuanian history.

The Kremlin's offers of appeasement had little effect on

Lithuanian nationalism. Calls for independence were intensified. On July 9, 1988, more than 100,000 Lithuanians attended
a rally led by the Initiative group in Vilnius. Banners were
displayed by the crowd demanding an end to Russian domination. In the past the voices of dissent were muted in response to
the Kremlin's harsh measures. During Stalin's rule, thousands
of Lithuanians who protested were sent to Siberia. In the
Gorbachev reformist era the demands for freedom became
louder and louder. Once again a disruptive nationalism was in
conflict with a centralized nationalism.

LATVIAN SEPARATISM. The Latvian S.S.R. was also a
small territory with important natural resources, occupying
24,805 square miles on the Baltic Sea. It has a population (1988
est.) of 2,673,000. Its capital is at Riga. Its natural resources
include timber and peat, and it produces dyes and fertilizers.
Like Lithuania, it gave the Soviet Union a highly desirable
access to the Baltic Sea.

The history of Latvia was replete with invasions of the
territory. The Livonian Knights conquered the country in the
thirteenth century and Christianized its people. Portions were
seized by Poland in 1561, by Sweden in 1628, and by Russia in
1721. In the eighteenth century, Latvia was dominated by
German merchants who were settled there by the Hanseatic
League and by German landlords. German barons maintained
control over Latvia until 1885. In the closing years of World War
I, Latvian patriots expelled both German volunteer bands and
Red troops. In 1920 peace was concluded with the Soviet Union.
Latvian independence was ended in 1940, when the Soviet
Union took over the country and transformed it into a Soviet
Socialist Republic.

In all this series of conquests the Latvian peoples never lost
their sense of identity. The Communist Party of Latvia, like its
counterparts in the other union republics, became the only
source of political power. The Party was dominated by non-
Latvians, mainly Russians and Slavs, propelled to power in the
Russification process. Nevertheless, Latvians worked to maintain their special cultural life. The national spirit was maintained by popular song festivals. Every five years the local

districts and towns held their own festivals and then sent their outstanding orchestras and choirs to the national festival held at Riga. Latvian literature flourished, including the national epic by Andrejus Pumpurs, "The Bear Slayer."

The Latvian people remain most concerned by the threatened loss of national identity engendered by Soviet control. The Kremlin favored the immigration of non-Latvians and used a harsh hand in throttling dissent. In the Gorbachev era, Latvians, encouraged by the new policy of openness, also took to the streets to reveal to the world their dissatisfaction with Soviet rule. Despite its efforts, the Kremlin was not successful in its policy of erasing nationalism in Latvia.

ESTONIAN DISSENSION. A spirit of grass-roots nationalism existed also in Estonia, then the Baltic S.S.R. With an area of 17,415 square miles, Estonia is the smallest of the three Baltic republics. Its population (1988 est.) is 1,571,000. Its capital city is Tallinn. Its economy is basically industrial, though there is some attention to agriculture.

The Estonians, linguistically related to the Finns, settled in their territory before the Christian era. In the thirteenth century, Northern Estonia was conquered by the Danes and the southern area by the Livonian Knights. The northern area was dominated successively by Sweden in 1629, by Poland in the same year, and by Russia in 1710 under Peter the Great. Along with its two neighbors, Estonia was incorporated into the Soviet Union in 1940 after the secret agreement between Hitler and Stalin.

After the conquest by the Soviet Union, nearly 90 percent of Estonia's industries were directed from Moscow. Most Estonians were restive under Soviet control and wanted to be free. (*See Reading No. 15.*) Estonia's proximity to Finland and its similar language contributed to Estonian dissatisfaction with Soviet domination. Several channels of Finnish television made Estonians easily see how their standard of living had deteriorated under Moscow's domination. In 1939, economic conditions in Estonia under the Kremlin's control depreciated to the Soviet stage, with interminable waits in line for soap, shampoo, yogurt, and all the products of a normal society. Estonians wanted relief from the Soviet yoke.

INCREASING RESISTANCE. Opposition to the Kremlin's domination continued to mount in the Baltic states in the late 1980s. The Baltic peoples were aware that the Russification process was an attempt to thwart their cultural identity, and they resisted it wherever possible. The Kremlin's minor economic concessions did little to allay the discontent. Baltic separatism remained a thorn in the side of the Russian bear.

Baltic intellectuals called for acute emphasis upon their own languages and culture. Their historians emphasized the traditions of a common past. Christians denounced the atheism of Marxism and called for revival of their religion. Peasants held strongly to their customs and folklore. Underground newspapers (*samzidat*) flourished throughout the Baltic republics. It was a typical case history of throttled nationalisms reacting against a harsh central nationalism.

BLOODSHED IN LITHUANIA AND LATVIA. For the hard-liners, army chiefs, and the K.G.B. in Moscow the projected reforms of President Mikhail S. Gorbachev were outrageous departures from Soviet policy. Thousands of demonstrators in Vilnius were shouting "Freedom" and singing "*Tautos Giesme*," the haunting Lithuanian national anthem. When Soviet satellites rebelled, Moscow sent tanks into Hungary in 1956 and Czechoslovakia in 1968. This was the accepted way of handling dissatisfaction. The Kremlin's decision on the Baltic republics—tanks and machine guns.

The first move came in Lithuania in early January 1991. Troops were sent in to Vilnius to enforce the military draft. Then, on January 13, came the crackdown. Under cover of a citywide blackout the tanks moved into downtown Vilnius. They plowed into a crowd of hundreds of Lithuanian nationalists outside the state radio and television complex. Some fifteen people were killed and several hundred injured. A clandestine, pro-Kremlin group, the National Salvation Committee, claimed to be the legitimate government. The Army banned demonstrations and strikes and named a military commander. There were similar developments in Latvia.

President Gorbachev, recently in 1990 awarded the Nobel Peace Price, apparently was outwitted by the hard-liners in Moscow. He blamed leaders of the separatist Lithuanian Parliament and their supporters for the bloodshed in Vilnius. In Moscow the Kremlin kept silent as thousands of protest marchers denounced the new mood of authoritarian crackdown and paraded through Red Square shouting "Shame!" What would happen throughout the country where separatist movements were emerging like mushrooms? Was the authoritarian Communist Party still the dominant force despite five years of change inaugurated by Gorbachev?

THE BALTICS WIN FREEDOM. By early September 1991 the Baltics had their independence back. With the failure of the rightist coup in late August, the three countries reclaimed their freedom from the rubble of the Soviet state. Lithuania had declared its independence in 1990, Estonia on August 20, 1991, and Latvia on August 21, 1991. The twelve-nation European community announced its recognition of the Baltics. More than thirty countries recognized the states as independent. The three Baltic states were now faced with the perils of nationhood. Their problem now was to free themselves from the grip of the more than 100,000 Soviet military, K.G.B., and Interior Ministry troops still based there.

CHAPTER 4

NATIONALISM AND
THE NEW RUSSIAN REVOLUTION

THE TRAIL OF FREEDOM REACHES MOSCOW. In the third week of August 1991, people throughout the world looked on in amazement as the old order surrendered in Moscow. Along with the United States, the U.S.S.R. was a superpower, the holder of 27,000 atomic warheads. Now the vast union of diverse nationalities plunged into cascading disarray.

There were extraordinary preliminary changes. Already the Berlin Wall was smashed down. Soviet satellites in Eastern Europe had broken away. The Baltic states were clamoring for independence. The two Germanies were reunited. One by one, ten of the fifteen Soviet republics were demanding freedom from the epicenter of control from Moscow. Now the Soviet people, at long last aware of the bankruptcy of communism, were calling for freedom. No longer in fear of their oppressors, they were on the verge of accomplishing a kind of miracle, the reversal of a thousand years of autocracy. For years they had been judged to be a passive people, willing to accept brutal rule from above.

In the past, any deviation from Communist rule had been wiped out by Soviet tanks. Those who witnessed the slaughter in China were convinced that it was only a matter of days before the Communist Party and the K.G.B. would crack down on the dissidents, who were expected to fade away before the tanks. Now, for the first time in seventy-four years of Communist dictatorship and centuries of Czarist autocracy, the dissidents promoted an epochal event in modern history.

When the rightist coup came, it lasted just three days. Citizens mounted the tanks and sent them back from the center of Moscow. Throughout the Soviet Union, huge masses gathered and demanded the end of communism. The coup was so badly organized and the people so determined that the coup began to collapse within several days. It became clear that the people were thoroughly fed up with the Communist regime and its inability to satisfy the needs of the people. They could no longer stomach the Communist Party officials who lived in splendor while the masses suffered. There was a new demand for democratization and even a market economy, under which the capitalists seemed to prosper. Statues of Marx, Lenin, Stalin, and other Communist leaders were toppled by angry citizens. The Russian tricolor was unfurled in Red Square.

Centrifugal forces were accelerating throughout the land. Boris Yeltsin, elected President of the Russian Republic, and Mikhail Gorbachev, unelected President of the U.S.S.R., became rivals in a situation which could polarize the country.

It was a remarkable event, clearly one of the turning points in world history. For the Russian people, who had long been miserable under an inept tyranny, it was the dawn of a new age.

Sovietologists, experts on the Soviet Union, were also astonished by the news. Virtually all of them predicted a dire winter of 1991–1992 as the suddenly freed people tried to adjust to a way of life they had never known. Experts denounced the Gang of Eight, those die-hard Communists, who had supported the coup, as guilty of stupidity and an oafish brainlessness. They were described as inept leaders who failed to seize control of all the centers of power and then paralyze the dissenters. Those who plotted the coup claimed constitutional legitimacy but could not bring themselves to act in the ruthless fashion displayed by Stalin in his execution of anyone he deemed disloyal to him personally. The plotters failed to shut down the country's television, telephones, and other communication centers. Most important, the coup failed because it was a discredited action in a new-style society. The conspirators failed to understand that there were now new, independent power centers in the country. With *glasnost*, independent intellectuals, journalists, and elected officials were too well-educated to be ruled in the stiff way of Stalinist tyranny. There were new attitudes toward authority and a new demand for the citizens to control their own destiny. The blundering leaders of the coup intended to restore obedience by a society already sensing the way to democracy. Instead, they cracked that society wide open. The central authority was crippled by its traditional incompetence and the shift of authority to the fifteen republics.

As the Soviet Empire began to fall apart, many of the outside experts began to see signs of trouble. Some predicted an inflation of some 1,000 percent as the economy was in the process of reformation. Others prophesied a dangerous shortage of food as its distribution was hindered by failure of the bureaucracy to deal properly with grain imports. Still others predicted a rise in crime as the K.G.B. and the local police lost authority.

THE THUNDER OF RUNAWAY NATIONALITIES. There were strong indications that the Soviet Union was facing serious problems of dissolution even before the failed coup of August 1991. The multinational composition of Soviet society meant difficulties for the central government of the Soviet Union and the Communist Party which formulated its policies. (*See Reading No. 16.*) The Communists spoke in favor of "national self-determination," but it was always an empty gesture. In the struggle between national centralization and widespread decentralization, the Party chose and supported strict centralization. Any sense of breakaway national consciousness in the republics was regarded as enormously dangerous for the political integrity of the state. It was deemed a critical necessity to curb or neutralize any such tendencies. Party leaders made it a point to retain centralized control by pitting minorities against one another. The basic problem, never quite solved, was to hold together a tangle of races, languages, and cultures. (*See Reading No. 17.*)

After its access to power in 1917, the Communist Party introduced an extraordinary propaganda machine whose goal was to convince the people that they were living in a workers' paradise. The Communist system was hailed as the wave of the future, as a model for the world. All the people, from youngsters to senior citizens, were drilled in the virtues of Marxism-Leninism. This view held that the U.S.S.R. must counter the envious capitalist nations whose aim was to destroy this shining light in a darkened world. First and foremost, the Soviet people were to remain completely obedient to the Kremlin's leaders, guardians of the truth.

Stalin and his successors therefore gave their first attention to the armed forces. The wants of the people, even simple necessities, came a long second to that of the military. In 1917, as a

means of protecting the state, the Communist leadership organized the Cheka, the first secret police force. Eventually, as
successors to the Cheka, the secret police grew into a staff of
400,000 officials dedicated to the task of defending Soviet
society against dissidents, against anyone who did not understand that he/she was living in a proletarian paradise. The secret
police played a major role in Soviet life. The Cheka was
followed by an alphabet soup of designations—G.P.U.,
O.G.P.U., N.K.V.D., N.K.G.P., and finally K.G.B. (*Komitet
Gosdaratvenny Bezopasnosti*) (Committee for State Security).
Those who expressed the slightest difference with Communist
ideology were consigned to the dungeons of the secret police,
beaten and violated, tortured into confessions, and then consigned to prisons, Siberia, or execution. Every Soviet citizen
feared the knock on the door in the middle of the night. The
regime of Stalin turned into a reign of terror.

History has its own lessons. A people held for too many years
with an iron grip will eventually explode in frustration and
anger. Witness the dramatic episodes of the French Revolution,
when the masses rebelled against a constricting, almost feudal,
society. The Russian Revolution of 1917 was another example of
a downtrodden people striking against the excesses of government. For more than seven decades the Soviet system, fueled by
propaganda and defended by the dreaded secret police and
powerful armed forces, maintained its power. At first there were
rumblings of discontent, then a slowly rising tide of opposition.
Much of the dissent was directed against the Communist Party.
More and more it became evident that the leadership was unable
to solve the economic problems of production and distribution.
Where much of the world became inured, despite setbacks, to
capitalist prosperity, the average Soviet citizen was condemned
to a miserable existence. The drugs of propaganda failed to
convince a disgusted people that they were living in a superior
society.

Increasing dissatisfaction emerged during the Gorbachev era
when the Soviet people, at long last, were granted a new policy
of openness. Whispers grew into loud roars. After decades of
suppression, angry citizens took to the streets and denounced
their Communist masters. There were calls for democracy, even

for a market economy. The noise of dissension reverberated throughout the country. In individual republics there were increasing demands for autonomy or independence, above all for relief from the Communist ideology, which just was not working. The so-called "dictatorship of the proletariat" was denounced as a sham, as a fraudulent deception. It was a revolutionary situation.

UKRANIAN NATIONALISM. For the Kremlin the most feared of the dissenting nationalist movements was in the Ukraine. One of the fifteen constituent republics, the Ukraine held a dominant place in the Soviet economy. With its 233,100 square miles, it is the third largest region in Europe. Densely populated (1988 est. 51,377,000) the Ukraine borders on the Black Sea, with Poland, Czechoslovakia, Hungary, and Romania on the west and southwest. Its capital is at Kiev. The Ukraine contains the chief wheat-producing area of the Soviet Union. There are large deposits of coal and iron. The Communist leadership regarded the Ukraine as the vital heartland of the country, hence its severe reaction against any notions of Ukrainian separatism.

The history of the Ukraine reveals a long and unending search for self-determination, the essence of nationalism, and independence. During the early Christian era, one invader after another, including Mongols, Goths, Huns, Avars, and Poles, moved into the Ukrainian steppes. Russians came in from the north and by the early nineteenth century managed to take over the territory. However, the Ukrainians were as much dissatisfied with Moscow's control as they had been by the domination of other outsiders. Agitation for national revival was intense and persistent. A secret political organization, the Brotherhood of Saints Cyril and Methodius, founded at Kiev, became the spearhead of Ukrainian nationalism. It called for a federation of Slavic states free of Russian control. The most popular apostle of Ukrainian independence was the poet Taras Gregoryvich Shevchenko (1814–1861), who won the accolade of "the Ukrainian Pushkin." His emotional poetry was devoted to the cause of Ukrainian freedom. He showed extreme compassion for the victims of Czarist injustice. In 1847, Czarist authorities sentenced him to compulsory military service and sent him to the Urals as a private soldier. Shevchenko never regained his health and died at the age of forty-seven.

In its early stage the Brotherhood was confined to intellectuals, but the sense of national consciousness soon gathered mass appeal. By the end of the nineteenth century the movement attracted solid labor support in the newly industrialized Ukraine. After the Bolshevik Revolution of October 1917, the *Rada*, the Ukrainian Council, proclaimed independence on January 22, 1918. Lenin, who previously had spoken in favor of the rights of national minorities, reacted violently. He opposed any recognition of Ukrainian national identity. The idea of Ukrainian independence was vetoed and the area was incorporated into the U.S.S.R.

During the Stalin era, the dictator made it his goal to stifle any notions of Ukrainian separatism. He denounced Ukrainian dissenters as "bourgeois national deviationists," dirty words in the Soviet vocabulary. He sent Nikita Khrushchev to the Ukraine with the special task of eliminating its leadership, a mission performed to Stalin's satisfaction. When Hitler declared war on the Soviet Union on June 22, 1941, his forces moved quickly into the Ukraine. Then the Nazi *Fuehrer* made a critical mistake. He treated the Ukrainians, many of whom preferred German to Russian domination, as Slavic beasts. The inevitable result was that the Ukrainians most reluctantly returned to the detested Russians and supported Stalin in his "Great Patriotic War."

The Ukrainian sense of national consciousness still had plenty of life during the post-World War II era. Angered by the Kremlin's iron control, Ukrainians both inside and outside the Soviet Union revived their campaign for freedom. A Ukrainian Insurgent Army (U.P.A.), operating from the Carpathian Mountains, began a guerrilla campaign against Moscow. The dissent became even more striking after the death of Stalin in 1953. A new generation of Ukrainian intellectuals emerged to renew the demands for freedom. They revived the passionately nationalistic poetry of Shevchenko. Their country, they insisted, had been deprived illegally of its independence; Ukrainian political and economic rights had been heavily limited; the Ukrainian language was banned; and many Ukrainians were disgusted with "Great Power Russian chauvinism." Hundreds of separatists were tried in secret for disseminating anti-Russian propaganda and were sent to labor camps. There were outcries against persecution and prosecution. Exiled author Aleksandr Solzhenitsyn condemned the policy of oppressing Ukrainians. Authorities in Moscow were adamant: they denounced Ukrainian dissenters as guilty of "an ugly strain of nationalism."

Ukrainian students joined in the campaign for freedom. Student militancy in October 1990 pushed the Communist-dominated Parliament into retreat and brought the nationalist movement into a more aggressive agenda. Thousands of students from all over the Ukraine rushed to Kiev to support the nationalists. For two weeks there were hunger strikes, marches, and demonstrations. Neither students nor older citizens could forget that millions of Ukrainians had been victims of the Stalin-engineered famine of the 1930s.

The confrontation continued with ill-will on both sides. Ukrainians claimed that their rights had been assured by the Soviet Constitution and by the 1975 Declaration of Human Rights signed by the Soviet Union. In turn, the Soviet authorities, besieged on all sides by calls for independence, called Ukrainian separatism as bare-faced treason that could lead to dissolution of the U.S.S.R. (*See Reading No. 18.*)

ETHNOCENTRISM IN MOLDAVIA. The Moldavian S.S.R., the second smallest of the fifteen constituent republics, had an area of 13,012 square miles. It is situated in the southwest part of the Soviet Union, borders Romania, and includes Bessarabia. It is an agricultural region, where grain and tobacco are grown. Its capital is at Kishinev. Its population (1988 est.) is 4,224,000.

The region was taken from Romania in 1940 and the Moldavian S.S.R. was established. After 1941, when the Soviet Union and Romania were at war, Bessarabia was seized by the Russians. In 1944, Soviet troops poured into the area and the Moldavian S.S.R. was re-established.

In the midst of the political confusion nearly paralyzing the Soviet Union, the Moldavians provided another serious problem for the Kremlin. Non-Moldavians make up some 36% of the republic's population. Moldavian nationalists denounced non-Moldavians as "enemies of the people." The majority applied to their ethnic rivals the same standards that Moscow used for them. The Kremlin saw its own power being demolished by ethnic rivalries. In Moldavia different groups and regions clashed repeatedly in attempts to assert their own nationalism and break away from Moldavian control. Dniester secessionists declared a separate Trans-Dniestrian Moldavian Soviet Socialist Republic. (*See Reading No. 19.*) In early November 1990 the tense situation in Moldavia turned to violence. Six people were reported killed and 30 wounded after vigilantes entered a predominantly Russian-speaking town in the republic's eastern region. Here a minority declared independence from Moscow.

Meanwhile, Moldavian nationalists continued their own campaign for independence. They issued a new flag, an upside-down version of the Romanian tricolor. The date of August 30, when Moldavian became the state language, was set aside as a national holiday. There was a switch from the Cyrillic to the Latin alphabet. The main boulevard, named after Lenin, was changed to Stefan the Great, a fifteenth century Moldavian prince. Contacts with Romania, which had been discouraged by Moscow, were re-established. The people retreated from Communist atheism; there was a strong religious revival as the number of churches increased eightfold.

Disturbed by the mounting ethnic rivalries, Moscow sent troops to maintain order. Crowds gathered to protest the "interference." Moldavians wanted no control from Moscow and no secessionists in their own midst. President Mikhail S. Gorbachev denounced what he called an alarming situation. He saw the integrity of the Moldavian republic as under threat. He urged Moldavians to rebuff the separatists and insisted that the republic would not be left in trouble. He did not add that his own regime was in difficulties.[1]

GEORGIAN SECESSIONISTS. Joseph Vissarionovich Dzhugashvili, better known as Stalin, was of Georgian—not Russian—origin. He was born in the provincial Georgian town of Gori in the Caucasus. Soviet propaganda made the house in which he was born an object of veneration. But Georgia itself

---

[1] After the end of the U.S.S.R. and the formation of the Commonwealth of Independent States, the new government of Moldavia changed its name to Moldova.

was never relieved from the power of this ruthless dictator, described by scholar George F. Kennan as guilty of incredible criminality. A twentieth-century Ivan the Terrible, Stalin impressed his will on an entire nation and destroyed its sense of individual freedom. Though he spoke Russian with a Georgian accent, he dismissed the idea of Georgian independence as grotesque nonsense.

The Georgian S.S.R. lay at the eastern end of the Black Sea, just to the south of the barrier formed by the Caucasus Mountains. The territory is largely mountainous and a large part is covered by forests. A relatively small area, it consists of 26,911 square miles. Its population (1988 est.) is 5,297,000.

Georgia has its own language and historical traditions. It is a long-standing Christian community. Stalin's mother hoped that he would enter the priesthood, a status he quickly rejected. Georgian history is a story of recurrent invasions, leading eventually to Czarist colonialism and finally to Soviet centralism. For centuries the Georgians had been dominated by successive overlords. But Georgian culture flourished in the twelfth and thirteenth centuries, as well as later. Shota Rystaveli's epic poem, *The Knight in the Tiger Skin*, became for Georgians a special expression of their national genius. Georgia was seized by Russia at the end of the eighteenth century. In May 1918, after the Bolshevik Revolution, Georgia proclaimed its independence, which was recognized by Moscow two years later. In 1921, Soviet troops entered the territory. In 1946 it was made a republic of the Soviet Union.

Georgians resented Stalin's policy of Russification. Intellectuals probed deeply into their past to find evidence of national cohesion. They crowded their universities with sculptures of Georgian poets and painters, and only rarely exhibited busts of Lenin. This was their way of emphasizing their own culture, which they insisted on retaining despite Stalin's efforts to hold them in line. The Soviet dictator was especially angered by the survival of Menshevik sentiment in Georgia. He saw Menshevism as dangerous as what he called deviationism of any kind. When in mid May 1972 the Georgian Institute of History, Archaeology, and Ethnography sponsored a book by Ushangi I. Sidamonidze titled *Historiography of the Bourgeois-Democratic Movement and the Victory of the Socialist Revolution in*

Georgia, 1877–1921, Soviet leaders reacted angrily. The author, they charged, had made too much use of Menshevik instead of Bolshevik sources. They would not tolerate that kind of alarming scholarship. This was "objectivism," condemned as unacceptable in the Soviet vocabulary. The author recanted, but was allowed to retain his Party membership.

Orders came from Moscow to keep Georgians under Kremlin domination. In November 1976 the Central Committee of the Georgian Communist Party, on orders from the Kremlin, issued a decree designed "to intensify the struggle against harmful traditions and customs." "Harmful traditions and customs" were seen as anything dangerous for centralized control of the country. The measure banned Georgian religious festivals, celebrations of saints days, arranged marriages, and "extravagant" wedding and funeral feasts. From Moscow's point of view there was entirely too much attention to religion, denounced by Lenin as "the opium of the people." For Georgians the measure was even more unpopular because it condemned the excessive drinking for which they had been known throughout the Soviet Union.

During the Stalin era the nationalist movement in Georgia remained muted. The people were cowed by the dictator's denunciations of localized deviationism. Few militants dared to risk Stalin's wrath. But gradually throughout the republic, as economic conditions worsened, Georgians began openly to express their desire for change. They, too, like others in the country, were incensed by the "new aristocrats," the Communist Party leadership. With the advent of the Gorbachev era, Georgians began to increase their demands for autonomy or independence.

The Politburo reacted as expected. Georgian separatists were denounced as "non-persons with twisted minds." Once again the Soviet Union was threatened by the heightening struggle between centralized nationalism and dissenters.

ARMENIAN RESISTANCE: ETHNONATIONALISM.

The Armenian S.S.R. was a landlocked, subtropical area just north of the mountain range of the Caucasus. The smallest of the fifteen republics, it occupied an area of 11,306 square miles. The territory is extensively irrigated. Copper, zinc, aluminum, and marble are mined. Its population (1988 est.) is 3,459,000. The capital is Yerevan.

The Armenian people have endured a tragic history. The Armenian sense of independence was tenacious throughout the centuries of conquest by Assyrians, Macedonians, Persians, Mongols, Turks, and Russians. Behind Armenian sentiment for nationalism were strong elements of identity—the Armenian language, literary and cultural traditions, and attachment to Christianity. The destiny of Armenians, especially under the domination of Turks and Russians, is linked to decimation and spoliation. They never lost their desire to be an independent nation.

Armenians regard their conversion to Christianity in 301 B.C. as the supreme event in their history. Later, they were subjected to control by other religions, but they never weakened in their loyalty to Christianity. They were restive under Ottoman domination in the nineteenth century, but at first were relatively docile. The Armenian bourgeoisie, taking advantage of the Industrial Revolution, tried to better their position under the Turks. Meanwhile, they stayed rigidly with their own culture. Poets, philosophers, artists, teachers, musicians, all adhered enthusiastically to their past and kept alive their sense of national identity.

Sultan Abdulhamid II saw Armenian devotion to their traditions as little more than treasonable activity. Starting in 1894 and continuing for two years, came the first series of Armenian massacres, which attracted global attention. In 1909 there was even more devastating slaughter, when 20,000 Armenians died in the Adana massacres. The killing continued during the course of World War I and in the immediate postwar years. It is estimated that up to a million Armenians died at the hands of the Turks, while many others were deported to the desert where they died.

Appalled by the harsh treatment of Armenians, the victorious Allies proposed to establish an independent Armenia, but the project was never successfully completed. Recovering their strength after the lost war, the Turks continued to hold the Armenians in bondage. Meanwhile, Armenians, much against their will, drifted into the hands of the Russians. In 1920 the victorious Bolsheviks proclaimed a new Soviet republic, and in 1936 Armenia became one of the fifteen constituent republics of the Soviet Union.

As expected, the Russians promptly renewed their campaign of Russification of the nationalities. Armenians reacted in the same way they had opposed Turkish control. They held to their language, traditions, and customs. They discouraged intermarriage with Russians. They did everything possible to discourage any attempts to link them with the Soviet way of life. They displayed their own flag—a gold hammer-and-sickle split by a blue stripe. On ceremonial occasions they made it a point to stress their own sense of identity. In May 1977 the Armenian dance ensemble performed its national dances in Victory Park, Yerevan, before a 150-foot statute of Mother Armenia. The dancers carefully faced the snow-capped peak of Mount Ararat, a beloved Armenian symbol never forgotten. In a country devoted to Lenin's atheism, Armenians baptized their children into Christianity and enthusiastically attended their many churches.

The Armenians never forgot the Turkish massacres of their people, which they called "the Hundred Years' War." Armenian death squads operated throughout the world to strike back at their Turkish oppressors. They gunned down Turkish ambassadors in a long-remembered vengeance. From 1975 to 1981 there were some 136 attacks on Turks in what Armenians regarded as answers to the genocidal slaughter of their people.

Armenian opposition to Moscow increased during the Gorbachev era and its new policy of openness. In 1988 occurred one of the largest demonstrations against the Kremlin in the more than seventy years of the Soviet Union. Tens of thousands of Armenians marched into Yerevan and demanded that the Nagorno-Karabakh region be incorporated into Armenia. This was an Armenian area inside Azerbaijan, where Christian Armenians were in conflict with Muslim Azerbaijanis. Armenian nationalists insisted that the area was inhabited mostly by Armenians and that it be united with Armenia. Gorbachev, faced with similar problems elsewhere, ruled that the redrawing of borders was unnecessary and in any event such an action was "abuse of democratization." He said that any such step "would poison public mentality with nationalist venom and thereby spoil relations between the people for many, many years to come." Moscow would recognize reforms, but not localized border changes. Armenians were not appeased.

ATOMIC DISUNION. Disaffection in the Baltic republics and in the Ukraine, Georgia, and Armenia was only a part of a nationwide trend. By the end of 1990 the demand for relief from Communist control had extended to fourteen of the fifteen constituent republics. There were indications that the dizzying pace of disunion might be unanimous. Kirghizia, in the eastern part of central Asia on the border of China, was expected to join the fourteen other republics in demand for change. Even the Russian Soviet Federated Socialist Republic (R.S.F.S.R.), with its capital at Moscow, had joined the demand for district autonomy. The largest republic in the union, stretching from the Arctic to the subtropics and from the Polish border to the Pacific, contains 147 million people in the country's 286 million. Its new leadership put into effect a 500-day economic plan of its own and wrote its own constitution. But the R.S.F.S.R. soon had its own problems, including dissatisfaction of its own Tatar minority. (*See Reading No. 20.*)

The urge to break away was developing into a stampede. Apparently, the Soviet Union as it existed for decades was in danger of a new revolution, a change as important as that of the Bolshevik Revolution of 1917. Everywhere there were demonstrations and marches to show the anger of a people thoroughly fed up with Communist propaganda. Party bosses were thrown out of their jobs. No longer was the Communist line accepted as simple truth. The new Moscow City Council followed the mood of the people in rejecting a spurned ideology. It changed the name of the Lenin station in the southwest quarter of Moscow to Ysaritsyne. The name Marx Prospekt was eliminated. Dzerinsky Square, a hated spot because it faced the headquarters of the old Cheka secret police, was renamed Lubyanka Square. Most astonishing of all was the introduction of Western names. Two small squares were named for Charles de Gaulle and the Rev. Martin Luther King, Jr.

In the past the goal of Kremlin leadership was simple and clear-cut: any opposition by the nationalities was regarded as treason and was to be throttled as bourgeois deviationism. Even

the satellite states in Eastern Europe were brought into line by
Soviet tanks. The policy was hard; the nationalities were fused
in a single citizenry and were to be maintained that way. The
Soviet Union was to be a multi-cultural entity ruled from
Moscow, and it would be maintained by force.

The new crisis left the Communist functionaries perplexed
and bewildered. This was a totally unexpected turn of events.
The Soviet regime had long been successful in dominating its
nationalities. According to historian Hugh Seton-Watson the
long-range aim of the Soviet regime was a war of extermination
against the principle of nationality. Now the situation seemed to
have passed beyond the control of the centralized authority. The
issue was critical. Would the military be sent on a campaign to
enforce obedience? A frustrated people yearned for democracy,
self-determination, and a revised economy. Discarded Communists predicted chaos, anarchy, perhaps civil war.

The issue came to a critical head in late August 1991 when the
three-day coup by Communist leaders resulted in a fiasco. In
Moscow an angry mass of people turned back invading tanks
and for the first time struck a resounding blow for democracy.

THE NEW COMMONWEALTH. The year 1991 was cru-
cial in the history of the Soviet Union. By late December 1991 it
became obvious that Gorbachev's attempt at reform to save
communism, not destroy it, had failed. Acting on their own, the
three Slavic republics of Russia, Byelorussia, and Ukraine,
founding republics of the old union in 1922, established a
Commonwealth of Independent States to replace the U.S.S.R.
The new Commonwealth swiftly gained additional members, as
Kazakhistan and the four Central Asian republics decided to
join. The new capital became the Byelorussian city of Minsk.

The loosely knit Commonwealth plunged into a desperate
race with hunger, cold, and scarcity. Half the country's airports
were closed because of severe shortages of fuel. Food was
critically short in Moscow and St. Petersburg. There was panic
buying as citizens were faced with a runaway ruble.

Boris Yeltsin, Russian President and the leader behind the
Commonwealth, emerged as the dominant figure in the political
arena. Whether he can solve the critical problems or whether the

country descends into anarchy and civil war remains to be seen. (*See Reading No. 24.*)

For the government of the United States, the astonishing developments in the old Soviet Union meant that the United States had won the Cold War. U.S. policy now hinged upon the critical question of how to prevent the return of aggressive nationalism in the new Russian Commonwealth.

CHAPTER 5

THE TRANSFORMATION OF NATIONALISM IN GERMANY

CHANGE IN INTENSITY OF NATIONALISM. The vehemence of nationalism may change under historical circumstances. Germany and Japan, both ravaged by strong nationalistic fervor, were soundly defeated in World War II and lost millions of men in the conflict. In the postwar years both cast aside their aggressive behavior and turned their attention to peaceful economic pursuits. In the process they moved into prosperity and set an example for other nation-states.

The examination here will place stress on West Germany. It went on to become a leader in global economic life, while East Germany, mired in the awkward and paralyzing restrictions of communism, sank to the level of the Soviet Union. Both were careful to retain characteristics of national pride, the essence of nationalism. Both parts were reunified in late 1990.

THE COURSE OF GERMAN NATIONALISM. Nationalism played a vital if tragic role in German history. German nationalism started in the early nineteenth century as a protest against Napoleonic aggression, but at the same time it had cultural overtones. After the mid-century it was shaped by the policies of Otto von Bismarck. By the end of the century and at the opening of the twentieth century the German people had been led into the kind of national aggression which much of the world had to strike down. Behind German aspirations was a compounding sense of national consciousness which led the people to look beyond their borders for expansion. (*See Reading No. 21.*)

German nationalism was born in the darkness of Napoleonic despotism. The attempt of the Corsican to spread the ideas of the French Revolution, as he interpreted them, into the Germanies by force of arms provided the spark which ignited the fires of nationalism. The Germanies had been a medieval hodgepodge

until Napoleon gave them a boost toward unity by wiping out
most of the small principalities. To forget their humiliation,
Germans turned to their past, when the glorious German Empire had been the cockpit of Europe. They were attracted by the
contemporary movement of romanticism, and they sought for
an organic community wrapped in the old cloak of tradition.
They would mobilize their heroic past, with its folk songs, fairy
tales, sagas, and poetry, and place the accent on imagination
instead of reason. The tone was set by Johann Gottlieb Fichte in
his *Addresses to the German Nation*. Friedrich von Schlegel
expressed the idea: "Awaken Germans from stupor and shame
and ignominy! Awaken and act for the sake of German honor!"
The new national enthusiasm was expressed vigorously by the
Freikorps (patriotic volunteers), Friedrich Ludwig Jahn's
Turnerschaften (gymnastic societies), and the *Burschenschaften*
(student fraternities).

However, in this early stage of German nationalism the tenor
of the movement was set by Johann Gottfried von Herder (1744–
1803), historian and social philosopher. According to Herder,
the human race is a unit in which all nations could dwell in
harmony for the cultivation of humanity. Again and again he
stressed the ideas of national individuality and national character. It was this view which led German intellectuals in 1848 to
espouse the cause of unity on the basis of liberalism. They failed
miserably.

Instead, German nationalism changed from its quiescent,
cultural stage to an altogether different character. This was the
work of Otto von Bismarck. Aristocratic, conservative, mili-
taristic, and monarchist, Bismarck had no use for "phrase-
making and constitutions." In 1862 he made it plain that the
honeyed words of liberals were unacceptable and that progress
could be achieved only by "iron and blood," later changed in
popular usage to "blood and iron." (*See Reading No. 22.*)
Bismarck, as pointed out by Otto Pflanze, fostered the tradition
of the *Tatmensch*, the man of deeds who manipulated the reins of
power and was responsible only to his conscience for the results.
By synthesizing nationalism, autocracy, and militarism, Bismarck, perhaps unwittingly, contributed to a dangerous milieu.
By his three wars of unification, against Denmark in 1864,
Austria in 1866, and France in 1870–1871, he brought Germany

to a late national unification. The German people enthusiastically followed his lead. With unification Bismarck decided
that Germany was satiated and he turned his energy to the
problem of maintaining the peace. By this time he had won
world renown. Erich Eyck attributed not only German unity but
also the great landmarks of German history from 1860 to World
War I to Bismarck. Eyck also believed that the German Chancellor was responsible for the transformation and mentality of
the German people.

To his great astonishment, Bismarck was forced to resign in
1890 by the youthful and belligerent Kaiser Wilhelm II. Loud
and boisterous, the new emperor was dissatisfied with Germany's role as a world power. He wanted African natives
parading in the streets of Berlin and he desired a Big Navy to
rival that of Great Britain. His grandmother was Queen Victoria, but he was convinced that the British had gathered too much
of the world's soil and he wanted a place in the sun for Germany.
His bellicose sense of nationalism led him straight into the abyss
of World War I. Mesmerized by their ambitious monarch, his
people, from labor to the intelligentsia, supported him. (*See
Reading No. 23.*) Millions of human beings were slaughtered in
that ghastly war. It took a coalition of Allied powers to drive
Wilhelm II into exile and his people into defeat.

The Germans were not happy with the results of that war. In
1918, with the end of the conflict, not a square inch of German
territory was held by the victor powers. Dissatisfaction was
widespread. There stepped into the picture a wild-eyed Austrian
politician, who declared that the Treaty of Versailles was an
outrageous fraud and that the war had been lost because of the
machinations of Social Democrats and Jews in Berlin. With a
pounding propaganda machine, utilization of bread-and-
circuses, and a constant stress upon national pride, Adolf Hitler
won the support of the German people. He would rectify what
he called the evils imposed upon an innocent Germany, and he
would lead Germany to its rightful place in the sun, which had
been denied by the Allies in World War I. Once again, the
German people were mesmerized by a political leader impelled
by an aggressive nationalism. His national state, he thundered,
would last for a thousand years. He led it confidently into
another war. But his National Socialism lasted for only twelve

years. Millions of Germans were sacrificed in the cause of blatant, bellowing nationalism.

Before they were aware of it, the German people were trapped into a harsh dictatorship. Enemies of National Socialism, especially Jews and Gypsies, were consigned to gas ovens in extermination camps. The name of Germany was forever besmirched by a barbarous regime, unique in the history of civilization. Only a small core of dissenters fought the Nazis inside Germany. They knew that they were placing their lives in jeopardy, and, indeed, most of them were executed. Again, it took a global combination of powers to bring down the Nazi dictator, who had transformed the Germany of Beethoven, Bach, and Brahms into the Germany of Hitler, Himmler, and Hess.

By 1945 the German people had learned much about the dangers of aggressive nationalism. Their cities were smashed into ruins, their Nazi leaders brought before an international court and then executed for war crimes, their people clothed in misery. Then, slowly but surely, the Germans began to recover from the evils of Nazism.

ON THE GERMAN NATIONAL CHARACTER. The idea of national character has engaged the attention of observers of the German scene. (*See Reading No. 1.*) They describe the concept as formed by the totality, traditions, and ideals which are so widespread and influential in a nation that they mold its image both in the minds of its people and in the minds of others. It is claimed that national character is a strong element in every nationalist ideology. Some observers even hold that national character is permanent, that it is built up over the course of time and retains its hold over a people.

Opposed to this view is the equally strong belief that anything concerned with national character is simply fallacious and incorrect. National character, it is said, just does not exist. Those who hold this view charge that the concept of national character is based on stereotypes and generalities. It exaggerates such stereotypes that all Frenchmen are amorous, all Scotsmen frugal, all Swedes cold, and all Americans aggressive and naïve. To this is added the ideas that every German yodels, eats *Bratwurst*, drinks beer, and wears *Lederhosen*. Critics maintain that the idea of national character must be rejected entirely as illusory. (*See Reading No. 2.*)

Between these two extremes is the view that national character has a limited validity because its existence cannot be denied. German historian Leopold von Ranke accepted this reserved attitude when he stated that the national spirit could only be felt but not understood. He saw it as a spiritual air, permeating everything. This moderate view was also held by Max Hildebert Boehm, who recognized national character as one of the most significant factors in the more precise and pronounced elaboration of modern nationalism. He suggested that the ideas that peoples have a common character and that national characteristics are possible were very old and ineradicable. He pointed to the impressions gained by travelers during visits to other countries. In his view, those who criticize the acceptance of national character have not distinguished clearly enough between the various aspects of the problem. He admitted that national character cannot be defined exactly or determined. He recognized at least a relative uniformity and consistency in the citizens of a nation. He suggested that the determination of national character is rendered more difficult because there are also common attitudes characteristic of the age as well as groups and individuals. It followed that national character is a partial factor in the lives of people, even though it is difficult to isolate it and describe it adequately.

Boehm also commented on the immutability of national character. He believed that socially dominant characteristics are historically justifiable and that the historical identity of a people is not destroyed by such change. A complete constancy of national character, therefore, cannot be maintained. He regarded single characteristics of a people as showing extraordinary powers of survival and self-assertion.

. The Boehm analysis may well be applied to the course of German history. German romanticists, especially Georg Wilhelm Friedrich Hegel, developed the theory of the *Volksgeist* (national spirit) as a metaphysical hypothesis whereby the history and culture of a people can be traced to a common root. Hegel turned from the Western rationalists and their glorification of liberty, equality, and fraternity, and opted for the obe-

dience of the individual to the state. Where Herder had stressed
the cultural aspects of the national character, Hegel chose
glorification of the state as the real goal of the German people.
By the end of the nineteenth century, virtually all teachers in
united Germany were Hegelian trained. The critical idea of
obedience to the state came to be a primal element in the
German national character. It was obvious that difficulties
would arise when those in control of the state provided the
wrong kind of leadership. Both Kaiser Wilhelm II and Adolf
Hitler were legally admitted to power. As obedient citizens,
Germans supported those who held the reins of power.

Most scholars today reject the idea that national character
exists permanently. On the contrary, the sentiments of a people
change according to historical circumstances. The Germans
provide an excellent example of the tendency of national character to display the temper of the times. In the early nineteenth
century they were regarded as a gifted, relatively peaceful
people dominantly concerned with their cultural attributes. By
the end of the century, in response to their leadership, they
emerged as a warlike community bent on conquest. They were
not content merely to watch the global successes of the British
Empire. They, too, wanted the spoils of colonialism and imperialism and were willing to respect their leadership in the desire
for a place in the sun. Obedient, submissive, apolitical, militant, they followed their leaders into the abyss of two World
Wars. They were fated to learn the calamitous lesson of too
much reliance on obedience to flawed leadership.

The German national character reflected the course of German history. Outstanding has been a polarity of ideas and
procedures that have never been resolved. The history of the
Germans has been a story of the struggle for a working compromise between uniformity and disruption. Uniformity is contrary
to the ethnic, political, and cultural divergences of the Germans. Seldom in German history has there been one central
power strong enough to crush the centrifugal tendencies of the
component parts. At no time were the individual parts weak
enough to allow themselves to be merged for a long time in one
highly centralized body, with the exception of the Third Reich.
These historical tendencies had an effect upon the nature of the
German national character. In his *The Course of German History*

(1946), the British scholar, A. J. P. Taylor used his mellifluous style to describe the dualities in the German national character. "The history of the Germans is a history of extremes. It contains everything except moderation, and in the course of a thousand years the Germans have experienced everything except normality." (*See Reading No. 25.*)

In his *The Mind of Germany* (1960), Hans Kohn, pioneer scholar of nationalism, described the change in the German national character. The Germans, he wrote, have been fascinated by the concepts of *Geist* (spirit) and *Macht* (authoritarian power). In the late eighteenth century they underrated the importance of power and overrated purity of spirit. In the nineteenth century the German attitude changed from one extreme to another. While remaining fundamentally apolitical, the Germans became a dynamic nation whose will centered upon power and the power-state. They turned to the pursuit of power, in the course of which they overestimated it. They rejected the critical control of power by spirit and idealized the power-state. The work of Hegel was devoted to this idealization of the state. This was a conscious deviation from the main lines of Western development, with its accent upon democracy and Rousseau's will of the people. This turn from spirit to power was to have a tragic effect not only for Germans but for the rest of the world.

ANOTHER CHANGE IN NATIONAL CHARACTER. The catastrophic defeat of Germany in 1945 left the German people scarred and disillusioned. The recovery which began in 1945 was marked eventually by another drastic change in national character. The aggressive attitude of the past was rejected as Germans began to rebuild their cities and their society. The practice of integral nationalism had brought them little other than misery. They now turned their talents to the pursuit of economic interests. Within four decades, the new democratic state of West Germany emerged as one of the most prosperous nations on earth. The German lust for political power was thrown aside, and it was succeeded by a policy of work, work, and work. For the rest of the world it was an economic miracle. It was, indeed, a remarkable development in German history. The new democratic Federal Republic became a part of the Western community. Only a short while ago the Germans had been a deadly threat to this community; now they joined it as a respected member of world society. Out of the chaos of World War II came a new Germany taking an honored place on the world scene. It rejected the fall into Nazi barbarism.

REUNIFICATION AND THE NEW GERMAN NA-TIONALISM. By 1990 the reputation of the German Federal Republic for decency, justice, and fairness was so great that the victor powers agreed to the reunification of the two German states. The German Democratic Republic, set up at the end of World War II, had a Marxist government favored by the Kremlin as a bulwark of communism against the capitalist West. Though East Germany was presented as an ideal Communist state, like the Soviet Union itself it was beset by Marxism in disarray. The Communist ideology just was not working, either in the Soviet Union or in the German Democratic Republic. In the late 1980s conditions in both countries worsened drastically to a point where both peoples began an agonized call for change, even for the beginning of a market economy.

On November 9, 1989, over twenty-five years after the Berlin Wall was built, it was smashed down and the peoples of the two Germanies were reunited. There were tumultuous scenes in Berlin, where half a million East Berliners and Eastern Germans converged in the western half of the city. It was an unprecedented mass demonstration as the people rose to challenge the authority enjoyed by the Communist Party. Thousands of West Berliners welcomed Eastern pedestrians with open arms, champagne, flowers, and tears of joy.

The reunification of the two parts of Germany was officially recognized on October 3, 1990. On the eve of the treaty for the final settlement, Hans-Dietrich Genscher, Minister for Foreign Affairs of the Federal Republic, greeted with joy the reunification of Germany. (*See Reading No. 26.*) The German people were delighted. (*See Reading No. 27.*) Europeans accepted the change. (*See Reading No. 28.*) British jurist Lord Shawcross saw Germans as a now different people. (*See Reading No. 29.*) Americans expressed wide support but added a note of caution. (*See Reading No. 30.*) Journalist William L. Shirer judged the Germans to be a people of extremes. (*See Reading No. 31.*)

EVIDENCE OF CHANGE. There is little doubt that the Germans feel the burden of their past. There has been a tremendous change since the era of Hitler, when the German name was cursed throughout the world. During the Nazi rule, German soldiers fought on the soil of more than half the European states. Unspeakable crimes were committed in the name of National Socialism. Now, after a long historical struggle for popular freedom, the Germans were filled with a sense of history and responsibility.

Most of all, during the forty-five years of the postwar era, the German national character again underwent a critical change. This is substantiated by attention to the German press during the last several years. These reports reveal a striking transformation in sentiment despite expressions of caution.

Item. Ceremonies were held in West Berlin and the Federal Republic in memory of the victims of *Kristallnacht* (Night of Broken Glass), November 9, 1938. The Berlin Mayor declared that the terror of the destruction of synagogues and Jewish businesses by the Nazis during that night was able to take place because "mental walls had been erected in the hearts and minds of people." (*This Week in Germany*, German Information Center, November 11, 1987.)

Item. An international youth center near the site of the former extermination camp of Auschwitz, Poland, was a host to 1,300 young people and was constantly filled to capacity during the vacation season. (*This Week in Germany*, December 11, 1987.)

Item. The director of the State Judicial Authorities for the Investigation of National Socialist Crimes in Ludwigsburg (Baden-Württemberg) predicted that numerous Germans accused of Nazi war crimes will face trial in the coming years. It was a new wave of investigation. (*This Week in Germany*, January 8, 1988.)

Item. The German Bundestag unanimously agreed to approve a plan for the establishment of a memorial for the victims of National Socialism at the site of the former concentration camp in the Drütte District of Lower Saxony. (*This Week in Germany*, November 24, 1989.)

Item. At the first conference of the World Jewish Congress held in Germany, Federal Chancellor Helmut Kohl called for war on anti-Semitic prejudice and for a close and confidential dialogue with Israel as the mainstay of the policy of a United Germany. The German people, he said, must always support Israel, which has arisen from the ashes of Nazi persecution of Jews. (*Süddeutsche Zeitung*, Munich, May 8, 1990.)

It is obvious that there has been a tremendous change in Germany since the Nazi era. The history of Germany has been a long, disappointing voyage toward the light of freedom. It started with German romanticism rejecting the Western Enlightenment. Over the course of the nineteenth century the national character was transformed into belligerence. The way Germany was united in 1871 was dangerous for the future. The descent into militancy in 1914 and the continued urge for dominance in 1939 left grave repercussions.

Contemporary Germany is a far cry from the Germany of the nineteenth century. It has discarded the disagreeable nationalism of its past performance, and it is generally agreed that the new Germany has changed in the nearly half century after the close of World War II. It is now a prosperous, working democracy stripped of the evil side of nationalism. Its people are aware of the monstrosities of Nazism and have rejected it in favor of a proud cultural nationalism. Admittedly, there has been a worry for Germany in a resurgent nationalism, primarily among skinheads and dissatisfied youth in Eastern Germany. This kind of neo-Nazism is rejected by most Germans as an unwarranted return to a disgusting past.

CHAPTER 6

ETHNICITY AND
THE MINI-NATIONALISMS

ETHNIC RIVALRIES. Historian Arthur Schlesinger, Jr. correctly judges ethnicity to be one of the most important issues of the day. He sees the history of the world to be in great part the mixing of peoples of differing origins, languages, and religions, inhabiting the same locality and living under the same political sovereignty. There is growing ethnicity throughout the world, even in stabilized nations.

The result of this growing cult of ethnicity has been a clash between two forms of nationalism: the centralized state, seeking to hold its ethnic components together, and mini-nationalisms attempting to assert their own identity through freedom from the center. Both forms are aspects of nationalism in action and both are growing in power and importance.

In the Soviet Union, with its plethora of more than one hundred nationalities, the state ruled from Moscow and did everything possible to control the dissatisfied minorities. This process is not peculiar to any one state. The minorities hold strongly to their own language and culture, retain their opposition, and yearn for the day of freedom, autonomy or independence.

Scholars have given these dissenters varied names—ethnic groups, nationalities, separatists, regionalists, and mini-nationalisms. They may differ in minor aspects, but there is a common thread in all of them, the desire for freedom from the central authority and the right to establish a new nationalism of their own. Some remain relatively mute, as for example the Welsh and the Scots, who accept the unity directed from London. At the same time, they place strong accent upon their own language and cultural manifestations while bowing to political domination by the centralized nationalism. The situation is different in Ireland, where the Irish Republican Army, intent on independence for the entire island, wages a bitter campaign of terror against British control, including the assassination of Lord

Mountbatten and an attempt on the life of Prime Minister
Margaret Thatcher. Like dissatisfied nationalists elsewhere,
members of the I.R.A. consider themselves to be national
heroes fighting a war for liberation, and not terrorists devoted to
bomb and bullet as a means of winning their hotly desired
freedom.

Because of its widespread existence, the conflict between
centralized and local nationalisms has become a major factor in
modern history. It is one of the complexities of nationalism that
these two forms exists side by side in ever-increasing confrontation. It reveals how one form of nationalism may be directed to
union while another is geared to disruption. The mini-nationalisms may remain quiescent over decades. Centralized control
was maintained from Moscow both during the Czarist era and
the Soviet Union. At some point the nationalities become so
frustrated that not even the power of the armed forces could be
counted upon to hold dissatisfaction in check. Yet the power of
the Kremlin and the Communist Party to throttle local nationalisms throughout the Soviet Union was not able to maintain the
triumph of centralized nationalism.

ETHNICITY IN EASTERN EUROPE. Not only in the
Soviet Union but throughout Eastern Europe ethnic rivalries
were intensified in the last decade. The special case of plurina-
tional Yugoslavia will be treated in the next chapter. The
internal situation of Yugoslavia is only one of the problems
facing the entire area. Romanians and Hungarians living side by
side exist in a state of alert as each lays claim to the territory on
which they live. The bitterness between the two peoples has
existed for decades. Romanians refer to Hungarians as Mon-
golian vandals, who seek to destroy the Romanian state and
press humiliation on Romanians in their own country. The
Hungarians reply in kind. Romanians in Transylvania claim that
the Hungarians speak of democracy but complain that they are
making life for Romanians impossible. Hungarians believe that
Romanians want to drive them from a home where they have
lived for centuries. Many Romanians are convinced that Hungarians are secretly plotting to take back Transylvania, a move
they regard as little less than treason. In 1920, after World War I,

the Treaty of Trianon gave Transylvania to Romania. Hungarians ever since commemorated what they call "bloody Trianon" and intensified their hatred of Romanians. For their part Romanians regarded their red, yellow, and blue tricolor as well as other national symbols as sacred and denounced Hungarian nationalists as "enemies of the nation."

In March 1989 the war of words between Romanians and Hungarians was transformed into violence in Tirgu Mures in Romania, when the conflicting ethnic groups went to battle in the streets. From the surrounding villages peasants armed with axes, knives, and bats poured into town to face their rivals. In the clashes five people were killed and 269 were hospitalized. This kind of ill-will has caused an increasing flow of peoples from the areas of conflict. Ethnic Hungarians flee from the areas of Romania that are predominantly Romanian, while Romanians in spots where there is a majority of Hungarians drift toward more stable territory.

This kind of national resentment increased throughout Eastern Europe. The retreat of communism and new conditions of democracy and free speech have led not only to new migrations but also to accumulated ethnic resentment. Hungarians oppose not only their treatment by Romanians, but also by Slovaks and Serbs. In Yugoslavia, Serbs and Croats are at each other's throats. Czechs and Slovaks turn on each other with fury. Mininationalists throughout the area denounce not only the ruins of Communist internationalism but also other regionalists and nationalities. Scholars throughout Eastern Europe turn to the historical record for more reasons to hate other peoples. Unlike Switzerland and Finland, where a compromise has been made between varied ethnic groups, the peoples of Eastern Europe have drifted into local enmities that go far beyond mere distrust. In some cases the differences have existed only for decades, in others there have been centuries of enmities. The clash of diverse nationalities has resulted in a deplorable situation of instability.

UPSURGE OF THE MINI-NATIONALISMS. The clamorous complaints of ethnic mini-nationalisms have extended throughout the world and have challenged centralized nationalisms everywhere. This has become one of the most important historical phenomenons of our time. Even a brief survey of the character of the mini-nationalisms indicates the extent of a serious problem in the contemporary world. (*See Reading No. 32.*)

Behind the drive for self-determination is the decisive element of power. Both in the formation of nation-states and in the desire of ethnic groups for independence, power becomes the deciding element and the ultimate arbiter. Might, strength, potency, authority, these are the important goals. The existence or dissolution of the system of nation-states depends upon the outcome of the power struggle. Where the central authority maintains its strength militarily, politically, and economically, self-determination of its component parts tends to remain relatively quiescent. Where the fulcrum of power weakens, dissatisfied people will tend to break their bonds. The struggle for power between the centralized nationalisms and the ethnic nationalisms remains among the most difficult problems of our time.

On the surface France may seem to be a stable nation-state, unified, governed from Paris, and happy in its designation as "a nation of patriots." Charles de Gaulle, the ultimate patriot, expressed his pride in the nation: "Our country, with her tinted sky, her varied contours, our fields full of fine corn and wines and livestock, our industry, our gifts of initiative, adaptation, and self-respect, make us, above all others, a race created for brilliant deeds." (*See Reading No. 12.*) Throughout their history the French have regarded the idea of political centralization as sacred and a fact of life. To most Frenchmen the idea of dissolution of their country is equated with insanity. In their view, to be a Frenchman is in itself a mark of distinction. Paris is the queen city of the world, and nothing must be allowed to challenge the unity of the state. For the French government the home-grown mini-nationalisms, no matter what type, whether moderate or extreme, must be kept within bounds and must never be allowed to threaten the existence of the centralized authority. French dissenters may have all the freedom they want to march in demonstrations and shout slogans, but they are classed as crackpots and lunatics if they want to separate one square inch of sacred French soil.

Yet, the happiness of the French in the glory of their state is marred by the existence of ethnic mini-nationalists from mild to terrorist. There is a strong separatist movement in Brittany, the province in the extreme northwestern part of France. Geography plays an important role in the Breton way of life because the isolation of Bretons contributed to distinctive customs. The Breton background is strongly Celtic. The urge for independence persisted throughout the Middle Ages. In the nineteenth and twentieth centuries Bretons held fast to their own sense of uniqueness.

The confrontation between Breton regionalists and French centralists was intensified when orders from Paris decided that Breton schoolchildren were not to use the Breton language in primary and secondary schools. Intellectuals began to express their dismay about the survival of the Breton tongue. Breton militants accentuated the call for freedom from centralized authority. In 1966, the Breton Liberation Front (F.L.B.) denounced "French imperialism." Its program stated that the Breton people were oppressed, the territory of Brittany was occupied by foreign French military camps, and the very existence of the Breton language was discouraged by Paris. Bretons demanded full independence.

Breton tactics at first were on a minor scale and opposition was limited to handbills and wall graffiti to win attention. Soon the disaffection accelerated into full-scale guerrilla attacks. In early July 1978, Breton extremists planted a bomb at Versailles. When some 50,000 people came to the palace grounds to witness a fireworks display, a bomb exploded and left a huge hole in the floor of a hall devoted to Napoleonic art. There was angry reaction throughout France. It was one thing for Bretons to demonstrate in their own territory, but it was a serious matter to strike at the heart of French culture. For most Frenchmen it was outrageous and scandalous to threaten the state in this unacceptable way.

In the summer of 1980, Breton separatists protested against the intention of the central government at Paris to construct a giant nuclear plant in Brittany. Reacting angrily, Breton nationalists spread the site with garbage and broken bottles and blocked access roads with debris. For them the proposed plant was an abomination. They charged that the central government had lied to them and allowed them to remain poverty-stricken compared to the rest of France. The opposition continues.

Considerably more violent than the Breton desire for independence is the Corsican drive for freedom. Corsica, relatively small with 3,352 square miles, is an island in the Mediterranean west of Sicily, north of Sardinia, and south of the French mainland. With its strategic location, Corsica attracted the attention of various maritime powers, most of which limited their penetration to the coastal areas. Eventually, Corsica came under French control. Dissenters against French rule were divided into moderates who called for more autonomy, and militants who would settle for nothing less than independence.

Corsican separatists were unwilling to rely on democratic means to satisfy their nationalism. Organized for that purpose, the Corsican National Liberation Front (F.L.N.C.) chose terror in its campaign for liberation. It held that the violence it used was only a necessary and legitimate means to stop colonial aggression. It would reply to colonial suppression with revolutionary and popular violence. It was not an idle boast. In the late 1970s, terror by bomb attacks won the guerrillas the name of "wild Corsicans." French public opinion was alienated when in May 1979 the F.L.N.C. planted a powerful bomb in the Palace of Justice in Paris. By the end of the month, some twenty-two Corsican bombs had been set off in Paris. From January 1978 to July 1979, Corsican terrorists were responsible for 466 bombings.

By the opening of 1991, French officials became alarmed that Corsica might be sliding into ungovernability. The French government pledged to restore order after a new outbreak of separatist violence. In recent weeks three local politicians had been killed. Members of the F.L.N.C. held hostages at a southern tourist resort and started a new series of bomb attacks that destroyed forty vacation homes. They made machine-gun attacks on public buildings in which the French flag was the apparent target. The separatists insisted that they would achieve "a process of true decolonization."

The French Government reaffirmed its plans to grant greater autonomy to the island. France, they said, was a nation of patriots, not semi-patriots. Corsica, in their view, should be grateful for its connection with French glory. The separatists were not convinced.

The dissatisfaction of separatists was not limited to Brittany and Corsica. The French Basques at the Pyrenees joined their brothers across the border in Spain in their stubborn demands for independence. (*See Chapter 8.*) There were also separatist movements in Alsace and Languedoc, as well as in Réunion Island and in Guadeloupe. No matter what the size of the territory, in each case the desire for self-determination remained the same. It was always ethnicity against the larger nationalism.

FLEMISH-WALLOON RIVALRY. How two peoples of differing backgrounds, language, and culture can be welded unhappily in one national state is illustrated by the clash of Flemings and Walloons in Belgium. Here two ethnic groups, each maintaining its own characteristics, exist side by side. In the early 1980s the total Belgian population (1989 est.) of 9,891,000 was divided into two major ethnic groups, the Flemings 57 percent, and the Walloons 33 percent. The languages were Flemish (Dutch) 56 percent, French 33 percent, bilingual 11 percent, and German 1 percent. The Flemings live mainly in the north and west, the Walloons in the south and east. The Flemings are subjected to Dutch-German influences, the Walloons to French historical traditions. Although greater in numbers, the Flemings believe that they are not granted the constitutional rights necessary for their role in Belgian life. They want a greater share in political administration and economic life. On the other hand, the Walloons seek to maintain their dominant position in Belgian society.

In 1815, the Congress of Vienna, seeking to remake the map of Europe after the fall of Napoleon, combined Belgium and Holland into the Kingdom of the Netherlands. It was an unfortunate step to unite two peoples separated by political and religious differences. In 1830, responding to the winds of change coming from Paris, both Belgium and Holland declared their independence. Belgium was recognized as a constitutional monarchy. The new kingdom combined two essentially different ethnic groups, Flemings and Walloons, into one country. On November 11, 1917, a Council of Flanders proclaimed the independence of Flanders. The Allied victory in 1918 put an end to the proposed independent state of Flanders. Since then the two different peoples have been at odds about their status in the Belgian state.

It is obvious that a linguistic wall separates the Flemings and Walloons in Belgium. Flemings adhere strongly to their own linguistic tradition and oppose any attempts to thrust their language to second place. Written Flemish was virtually identical with Dutch. The Walloons prefer French forms. French was designated the official language of Belgium. This set off a feud that has been maintained to the present day.

The Flemish-Walloon linguistic rivalry affected every phase of political and economic life in Belgium. French became the language of the courts, education, medicine, and everyday life. Flemings resent the fact that French-speaking Walloons held most of the administrative and professional posts. They charge that Walloons are given preference in industrial employment.

Faced with what they considered to be a wholly unfair situation, Flemings demand that their language be placed on an equal footing with French. They insist that all state business be conducted in both French and Flemish; that more Flemish be used in elementary and secondary schools; that inscriptions on Belgian coins be in both languages; that Flemish be given equal status in scientific research; that Flemish-speaking units be permitted in the military; that bilingualism be recognized for all legal cases; and that Flemish courses be introduced into the universities.

There was an important economic rivalry added to this language war. Flemings in the north had long preferred farming and textiles, while Walloons in the south chose commerce and industry. Taking advantage of the situation, the Walloon middle class—manufacturers, merchants, lawyers, and teachers—was more successful than the Flemings in acquiring wealth. Walloons were further enriched by the discovery of new coal basins in their territory. A dramatic change occurred by the time of World War I. The port of Antwerp, in the Flemish area, began to prosper, while the Walloons suffered an economic depression due to exhaustion of their coal mines. Walloons began to see a diminution in their economic status. They resented "the upstart

Flemings." The Flemings, in their turn, saw the transformation as historically justified.

The bitterness between the two ethnic groups with separate languages continues to the present day. A Walloon aristocrat stated that one speaks Flemish only with one's servants. The differences varied from social ostracism to angry physical encounters. Belgian police were kept busy breaking up street fights between contending linguistic factions. Typical was the scene on August 11, 1965, when a hundred Flemings ostentatiously walked out of a church service in Ostend when a priest began the mass in French for the benefit of vacationing Walloons. Gendarmes had to drive through the streets in armored vehicles to break up the ensuing riots.

The central government tried appeasement to solve the ongoing confrontations. On October 2, 1980, after years of debate, a measure of regional autonomy was granted to the two ethnic groups. Local bodies took control of the economy, public health, urban projects, and cultural matters. The federal government retained responsibility for national defense, foreign affairs, education, finances, and justice. How much this effort to solve a long-standing problem will succeed remains to be seen. The embers of ethnic nationalism may burst into flame at any time. All past efforts to solve the linguistic confrontation have been unsuccessful. The small nationalisms inside the nation-states are as stubborn as the larger centralized nations that work to hold them in check.

JURASSIC NATIONALISM. The problem is global. Even small Switzerland, a country widely recognized for its unity in diversity, has had to face the issue of a discontented minority. The Swiss people, with their mighty franc and their banks as repositories for a large part of the world's wealth, seem on the surface to have a smoothly run society combining several ethnic groups. The country acquired its present borders in 1815, when the European powers proclaimed neutrality for the Swiss Confederation. There are four national languages: German, 72 percent; French, 20 percent; Italian, 4 percent; and Rhaeto-Romansch, derived from Latin, 1 percent. Two religions exist side by side: Protestant, 49 percent, and Roman Catholic, 49 percent. The government was decentralized, based on 3,050 communes fitting into twenty-three virtually sovereign cantons, each with its own constitution, legal system, administration, and budget. The national constitution referred to "the Swiss nation," to the dual sovereignty of the centralized state and its component parts, and to the residual sovereignty of the cantons. The cantons were given a wide degree of sovereignty. Federal law prevailed over cantonal law in matters of national security, rights of property, and freedom of trade and industry. All residual powers were cantonal.

Added to this political arrangement which recognized diversity in the state was an important economic factor. By hard work and thrift the Swiss have constructed a highly prosperous state and its citizens enjoy a high standard of living. Wealthy individuals all over the world have stored their money in Swiss banks because they trust the Swiss for silence in such matters. Added to this attraction is a low inflation rate.

With this record it might be assumed that Switzerland is free of ethnic rivalries and ethnic desires for more autonomy or independence. Yet, Switzerland, too, has a problem with a dissatisfied minority. Stretching along the western border is the Jura region, consisting of bleak, limestone folds. Those who live in this area, largely of Huguenot persuasion, have developed a reputation for their austere faith, frugal manners, and preference for the French language.

Jurassic nationalists are not altogether satisfied with their lot in a prosperous Switzerland. They claim they are not given the freedom provided by the national constitution. A movement known as the Jurassic Rally, consisting mostly of students, began to agitate for change. The protesting dissidents appeared before the Federal Parliament in Bern and some turned in their rifles while announcing that they would not serve in the army until their canton was freed. The government sent in a mechanized battalion "on maneuvers," but it did not go into action. The students denounced the move as "imitating the Russians." On December 11, 1968, some twenty-five young demonstrators broke into a joint session of the Bern Parliament and demanded a separate state for the Jura region. They waved Jurassian flags and shouted for a "Free Jura." They read a proclamation calling for a separate canton.

Although the Jurassic rebellion was comparatively mild, and certainly never reached the zealous stage of Corsican or Basque terrorism, it indicated the powerful desire of ethnic groups all over the world for autonomy, freedom, or independence. The strength of mini-nationalist sentiment is revealed when it can obtain footholds even in prosperous Switzerland, whose people believe they have really attained "unity in diversity." The little nationalisms everywhere prefer disunity in protest against the larger nationalisms.

CHAPTER 7

CASE HISTORY I:
SOCIALIST FEDERAL REPUBLIC
OF YUGOSLAVIA

HETEROGENEOUS COMPLEXITY. The Socialist Federal Republic of Yugoslavia provides an excellent example of how difficult it is to weld into one nation-state several disparate ethnic groups each of which has its own national aspirations. It is not the easiest of tasks to bring together in harmony ethnic units with their own language, traditions, and cultural characteristics. The business of loving-thy-neighbor is too much to expect from those burdened by distrust and contempt for others. Yugoslavia is situated in the turbulent Balkans, a region inhabited by many independent-minded peoples. It is more than difficult to bring into close or intimate union peoples who are essentially not alike. Yugoslavia, as elsewhere in the world, thus becomes the scene for a struggle between two kinds of nationalism—the centralized nationalism of the supposedly unified national state and the nationalism of the ethnic groups who seek freedom, sovereignty, and independence.

Contemporary Yugoslavia, with 98,700 square miles, the size of Wyoming, and a population (1989 est.) of 23,750,000, is situated on the Adriatic coast of the Balkan peninsula in southeastern Europe. For centuries the area has been overrun by outside peoples from Greece and Rome, Byzantium, and central Europe. Varied ideas and interests were planted, with the result that imprints were left by Slavic, Western, and Eastern peoples. Today Yugoslavia includes a mass of differing peoples. Among the varied ethnic groups are Serbs 33 percent, Croats 20 percent, Bosnian Muslims 9 percent, Slovenes 8 percent, Macedonians 6 percent, Albanians 8 percent, Hungarians 2 percent, and Turks 1 percent. Added to this hodgepodge are Germans, Ukrainians, and Czechs, as well as Austrians, Greeks, and Poles. There is no melting pot here.

It follows that languages, the essence of nationality, are different in this conglomerate nation-state. Serbo-Croatian, Macedonian, and Slovenian are all official languages. In addition, there are Hungarian, Albanian, and other languages. Most of the people speak Slavic tongues. Croats use the Latin alphabet, the Serbs the Cyrillic. There are religious differences. Yugoslavia is about one-third Roman Catholic, one-tenth Muslim, and the rest Eastern Orthodox. Added to ethnic and linguistic variations are severe conflicts between the religions. Of such diversity is a nation which the central authority seeks to mold into a happy union of peoples. (*See Reading No. 33.*)

RECENT HISTORY. Behind Croatian demands was a history of an overpowering desire for independence. (*See Reading No. 34.*) On June 28, 1914, when the Austrian Archduke Francis Ferdinand and his wife were assassinated at Sarajevo, the Austrian government blamed Serbia for the tragedy. That event led to the outbreak of World War I. With the collapse of the Austro-Hungarian Empire in 1918, the Kingdom of the Serbs, Croats, and Slovenes was formed from a host of former provinces. Peoples of differing backgrounds were thrust together in what was supposed to be a unified state. The name of the country was later changed to Yugoslavia. Peter I of Serbia was installed as king. He died in 1921 and was succeeded by his son, Alexander I, who was assassinated in 1934 by a Croat terrorist. Prince Paul, the Regent, was overthrown in March 1934 and was succeeded by Crown Prince Peter. When Nazi Germany invaded Yugoslavia in April 1941, Peter II was forced to flee the country.

Two groups of Yugoslavian Partisans rose in rebellion against Hitler. One, called the Chetniks, was led by Draja Mikhailovitch. Another was composed of Communist Partisans under the leadership of Josip Broz, later known as Marshal Tito. The struggle between the two Partisan leaders was bitter and deadly. Broz, supported by the Soviet Union and Great Britain, gradually obtained the upper hand. By the time the Nazis were driven from Yugoslavia in 1944, Broz had won control of the nation. He denounced Mikhailovitch as a traitor who had collaborated with Hitler. Mikhailovitch was executed on July 17, 1946, by the new Tito government.

REGIME OF MARSHAL TITO. Josip Broz, called Tito (1892–1980), was the unorthodox Communist who pushed his way to the dictatorship of Yugoslavia. The son of a blacksmith in a Croatian village, he fought in Russia with the Austro-Hungarian army in World War I. He served in the Soviet army in the Russian Civil War, 1918–1920. Returning to Croatia as a metal worker, he became a union organizer. Charged with being a political agitator, he was imprisoned from 1929 to 1934. When Nazi Germany occupied Yugoslavia, Tito emerged as leader of a Partisan force which fought not only against the German invaders but also against the Serbian resistance leader Draja Mikhailovitch. In March 1945 Tito became head of the new Yugoslav federal government.

By 1945 Tito controlled the Communist dominated National Liberation Front. He became Premier and Prime Minister of Defense and began his dictatorial rule. Immensely popular with the many elements of his people, he introduced his own form of communism and enjoyed a wide measure of support. Stalin, dictator of the Soviet Union, was not inclined to accept opposition from any Communist and especially from Yugoslavia, which he regarded as within the range of his own domination. Tito was adamant in maintaining his country's independence and he had no wish to be subservient to the Soviet dictator. Stalin adopted measures which he believed would bring Tito into line. He tried various means: economic blockade, border incidents, and even talk of invasion by Soviet troops. Tito was unimpressed. By standing up to Stalin, he won ever more support among the Yugoslav people. After Stalin's death in 1953, Soviet authorities decided to mend relations with the obstreperous Tito. Two years later, Nikita Khruschchev visited Belgrade and officially rejected Stalin's policy. He recognized Tito's position on the equality of states and his right to pursue his own road to Socialism. Tito was successful in achieving his goal. He had transformed Yugoslavia into an armed camp, his secret police worked actively in his behalf, and he purged any dissidents in the Communist Party who opposed him. He became the national symbol of "brotherhood and unity."

Tito understood well the divisive nature of his country. His main problem was to keep the squabbling ethnic groups under control of a centralized authority. He was, indeed, successful to a large extent during his regime. Inaugurating a policy of appeasement, he decentralized the administration without sacrificing control from Belgrade. He set up a federation, a joint and equal community of all nationalities in Yugoslavia. The confederation comprised six republics: Serbia, Croatia, Slovenia, Montenegro, Bosnia-Hercegovina, and Macedonia, and two autonomous provinces, Kosovo and Voyvodina. The idea held that the confederation and the republics would be two essentially equal and mutually dependent and interlinked social and political communities.

Tito's solution seemed to work well in a country weakened by ethnic dissensions. While maintaining an iron dictatorship in Belgrade, he resisted both western influence and Stalin's aim to keep him in an inferior status in the Communist world. This brought him popularity with his divided people. He was able to maintain a unified state despite grumbling discontent. He died on May 4, 1980. His posts as head of the collective presidency and director of the League of Communists were delegated to a rotating system of succession among the members representing each republic and autonomous provinces. But once Tito disappeared from the scene, the quarreling minorities returned to their bitter disputes and began again to emphasize the demands for self-determination. The calls were loud and strident, and there was no Tito to stifle them.

REFORM AND THE CONSTITUTIONS. Behind Tito's efforts to hold the national minorities in check was a series of reforms he inaugurated in constitutions specifically designed to satisfy the minorities. Originally, the first Yugoslav constitution (1946) was influenced by the Soviet constitution. Most of its rights were given to the central government as befitted the nationalism of the state. After breaking with Stalin, Tito decentralized administration as a concession to his minorities. On January 13, 1953, he was elected first President of Yugoslavia. In April of that year he enacted a new constitution for the Socialist Federal Republic of Yugoslavia. In 1971, constitutional amendments seemed well on the way to making Yugoslavia a loose confederation of semi-autonomous units.

Tito supported this minority appeasement policy until in

November and December 1971 there were dangerous demonstrations in Croatia. The riots were denounced by both the League of Communists and the army. In 1974 the League of Communists called for a revival of "democratic centralism" and a new emphasis upon party discipline. This demand led to a new approach by the Constitution of 1974, which created new conditions at both federal and local levels. In the interest of national unity, it abandoned the idea of representative democracy and replaced it by easily controlled delegations. The constitution actually supported a recentralization of political life, and it urged a greater vigilance of the authorities against dissent. The economy as well as the thoughts of the minorities remained decentralized. The minority ethnic groups still cherished their idea of autonomy.

INTENSIVE CROATIAN SEPARATISM. Opposition to Tito's centralized nationalism took several forms. On the one hand, there were the moderate intellectuals who emphasized the traditions that bound the Croatian people together. They organized the Matica Hrvatka, a cultural association centered in Zagreb and dedicated to the preparation of an ideological base for the secessionist movement by accenting every phase of the Croatian past. The group supported research to reveal the uniqueness of Croatian culture, published books and pamphlets, and encouraged regional Croatian folklore, customs, and songs.

Students joined intellectuals in the drive to set Croatian institutions apart from those of the centralized Yugoslav state. They charged that Tito's old Partisans, who had won independence for Yugoslavia, had changed into fat and lazy parvenus attracted by a consumer society. They heaped scorn on what they called "the sandwich generation," those between 39 and 50, as flabby and hypocritical. Demanding freedom from their oppressors, they called for an independent Croatia that would recognize their right to self-determination.

Croatian dissension did not stop at the moderate line. A third group rejected the mild cultural autonomy policy of the intellectuals and students as weak and spineless. They would fight the established regime with the terror they claimed had been used against them. Militant Croatian separatism was distinguished by its bitter and impassioned tone. In its view, Yugoslavia was

an imperialist state held together by force and violence. Separatists demanded "a free, democratic, independent, and neutral
Croatia." If not granted, they would rely on terrorism to win
independence.

Croatian separatists denounced Tito's propaganda for a
united national state as invalid and grotesque. They accused him
of betraying his colleagues of the Yugoslav Communist Party
leadership and liquidating them without pity. They claimed that
he had unleashed an unprecedented reign of terror. They
charged that he had played the superpowers against one another
and took as much as he could from both sides in order to
maintain his economically bankrupt state. They held that
Yugoslavia under the Tito imprint was an imperialist state held
together by terror. They said they would reply in kind.

The Croatian case was strengthened by strong support from
abroad. Many Croatians had avoided the wrath of Tito by
escaping from their homeland and living in other countries.
Endangered in their own environment, they stepped up their
opposition from abroad. Settling in the Federal Republic of
West Germany, South America, and the United States, the
Croats waged a spirited campaign against the Yugoslav government. In the United States alone some 100,000 Croatians lived
in areas of Illinois and Indiana. The Croatian National Council,
with its headquarters in Chicago, and the Croatian National
Congress carried on what they called "the national liberation
struggle against imperialist Yugoslavia." Militant Croats operated from both Canada and Australia. One group known as
Otpor ("Resistance" in Croatian) was founded in Spain after
World War II and operated throughout the world. These dissidents did not retreat from use of terror. In 1971, Croatian
activists assassinated the Yugoslav ambassador to Sweden.
Other Croatians hijacked an airliner and threatened to destroy it.
A Croatian attempted to kill the Yugoslav ambassador to Para-
guay, but mistakenly took the life of the Uruguayan ambassador.
Croatian terrorists were suspected of blowing up the main
terminal at La Guardia Airport in New York City.

Croatian militants stepped up their campaign for independence. In mid-June 1977, Croatians invaded the building hous-
ing the Yugoslav United Nations Mission in New York City, shot

one person, and then distributed leaflets. Later that year the U.S. Federal Bureau of Investigation looked into the matter of several dozen extortion letters written in Croatian dialects, signed by "Coordinator of the Operation," and sent to people in Chicago, Cleveland, and San Francisco. The letters aimed to raise funds for the Croatian separatist movement. In December 1978, two Croatian separatists were convicted of taking over the German consulate in Chicago.

On March 14, 1980, the Croatian National Congress in New York paid for a large advertisement in *The New York Times*, which denounced Tito as a murderer. The advertisement listed "only a few" of the crimes Tito had committed against the Croatian people. It was a passionate litany of grievances. (*See Reading No. 35*.)

DISAFFECTION OF SLOVENIA AND KOSOVO. Equally as dangerous for the unity of Yugoslavia was disaffection in the republic of Slovenia and the province of Kosovo. On December 22, 1990, in another strike at the union, Slovenes voted overwhelmingly in favor of independence. Although an approval of only 51 percent was needed for the plebiscite to pass, some 96 percent voted for independence and 4 percent against. Although the vote did not mean an immediate break with the other five republics and the two autonomous provinces, the plebiscite endorsed a plan to take gradual control of military, foreign, and monetary policies, now in the hands of the federal government at Belgrade. The country seemed to be disintegrating with its increasing instability. The federal government, dominated by Serbs, seemed helpless.

Added to the problem was the growing dissent in Kosovo, the province in the south. The area is populated by a majority of Albanians, who outnumber the Serbs and Montenegrins. Albanians are mistrusted by the other ethnic groups. They are badly paid and live in poverty-stricken communities, but this has not dampened their desire for self-determination. The Serbs, however, regard the area as the cradleland of their own nationalism. Albanians are arrested and imprisoned. Such ethnic rivalries continue to tear apart the peoples of a nation that Tito had held together in his iron dictatorship.

URGE TO DISUNION. It is seemingly impossible for the localized nationalisms to shed their prejudices and remain happily secure in a divided country. The urge to disunion was increased by that which happened in the Soviet Union and in Central Europe. The Soviet state founded by Lenin after World War I was expanded into Western Europe by Stalin after World War II. It was in critical disarray. In Central Europe the post-Hapsburg structure of nation-states, created by the Western democracies, destroyed by Nazi Germany, and revived by Allied victory, appears to be outdated. The vigilant minorities in Yugoslavia are encouraged by what seems to be a recasting of the European structure.

CIVIL WAR IN YUGOSLAVIA. The unlikely union of disparate republics began to disintegrate in Yugoslavia as ethnic sentiment clashed with national cohesion in the summer of 1991. Croatia and Slovenia declared their independence, whereupon Croat nationalists and Serb rebels came to grips in a bloody civil war. Tribal instincts came to the fore as the bitter struggle began with all its tragic consequences. The Yugoslav Army launched tank attacks on Croat villages. The Serbs claimed that the Croatian National Guard had opened fire on federal army units. Serbian irregulars left a vista of death and destruction while blasting Croatian homes and killing civilians. Thousands of women and children died in the massacres. West European nations and the UN attempted to mediate, but no attention was given to ceasefire after ceasefire. Peace plans were thwarted by divergent interests abroad, and peace initiatives projected by various European states failed. There was a lingering fear that the struggle between central nationalism and ethnic sentiment would spread elsewhere. With the old Soviet Union drifting to its own form of anarchy, Europe was in its most volatile condition since the close of World War II.

CHAPTER 8

CASE HISTORY II: BASQUE NATIONALISM

THE BASQUE SYNDROME. Outstanding among the many dissident nationalisms throughout the world is the case of Basque separatism in Spain. This fervent call for self-determination has little to do with moderation or willingness to compromise. In the words of the syndicated columnist George F. Will, "fervor has seemed a necessity of the national nervous system; perhaps Spanish formality seems to smother the ferocity beneath the shell of the nation's life." The Basque call for independence has behind it a long tradition of independence and a current willingness to devote to the task a large measure of terrorist tactics. Basque nationalists admit openly that they are engaged in a dirty war of killings and assassinations.

Basque terrorists heartily condemn the moderate call for negotiations as puerile and ineffective. They are convinced that their goal of freedom can be achieved only through bombs, grenades, and bullets. They judge the moderate stand as the way of weaklings and fools. They will have none of it. For them the only correct solution to their problem is found in the violence of the Irish Republican Army and the Palestine Liberation Organization. They support the methods of their own *Euskadi Ta Azkatasuna* (E.T.A.), whose immoderate terrorism has brought it global attention. In 1976, in just one year, E.T.A. activists killed some 114 Spaniards they regarded as enemies of their cause.

The Basque syndrome is characterized by force unlawfully used. It is a passionate, furious, and emotional reaction against those whom they accuse of holding them in bondage. The process is long-lasting and suffused with bitterness.

The Basque problem is divided into two parts on both sides of the Pyrenees. On the Spanish side are four Basque provinces in the north of Spain: Vizcaya, Guipúzcoa, Alava, and Navarra, with some 750,000 Basques. Three Basque provinces: Labourd, Basse-Navarre, and Soule, with about 150,000 Basques, live on contiguous territory in southwestern France. Although the two ethnic groups consider themselves to be bound by historical traditions, there is a difference in their attitude toward separatism: the French Basques remain relatively moderate, while the Spanish Basques have turned to extremism and violence as their way of objecting to Spanish centralized nationalism.

BACKGROUND. Basque separatism has behind it a long historical tradition of opposition to those who would hold them in subjection. In their early history they resisted the efforts of Romans and Visigoths to control their territory. For centuries the Basques south of the Pyrenees were brought under Spanish domination, but they, nevertheless, managed to maintain self-control through their own *fueros*, or local laws. In 1873, because of their pro-Carlist stand in the Carlist Wars, they lost that privilege. They have never forgotten it. Thereafter, their goal has been to regain their precious rights and to oppose the centralized authorities in Madrid.

A major factor in the existence of Basque nationalism is linguistic affinity. The Basques have held rigidly to their own language. They speak *Euskera*, one of the most distinctive of the non-Castilian languages. Complex, it relates to no other language. It is guttural, with its own special phonology, grammar, and vocabulary. This agglutinative tongue has fascinated linguistic experts. For Basques it has a special meaning: it is a mark of distinction and reflects their own emotional desire for the existence of a separate Basque nation-state.

Language is an important factor in the formation of Basque unity, but other cultural elements accent the notion of difference. Over the course of centuries the Basques developed their own cultural qualities—in dress, customs, and folkways, all of which they guarded against the inroads of "foreigners," especially Spaniards. They are immensely fond of choral singing. "One or two Basques are nothing much," they say, "but three Basques always form a choir." Their favorite game is *jai alai*, in which players use scoops attached to their hands to throw balls at high speed. Community games, held annually, are hotly contested. Theirs is a special way of life and they seek to alienate it from other regions of Spain.

During the Spanish Civil War (1936–1939), the Basque pro-

vinces formed an isolated Republican enclave, certainly because the Republicans gave them autonomy at the start of the
conflict. The Basque Republic, which they had wanted for
decades, lasted just eight months. The establishment of the
Franco regime and its harsh leadership was for the Basques a
long period of martyrdom. The dictator used his iron hand in
suppressing regional languages and culture. Basque separatists
were punished without mercy. Restrictions were introduced
against Basque education, press, songs, and dances.

MILITANT REACTION. Basque separatists reacted angrily to Franco's moves to hold them subservient to Madrid.
They denounced him when he proclaimed a "State of Exception" and ordered the Civil Guard to strike against the dissenters. Activists were arrested, subjected to torture, and executed for "military rebellion." It was a vicious struggle as
Basque nationalists turned to terror in their drive for freedom.
(*See Reading No. 36.*)

To avoid the Civil Guard and the secret police, some Basque
nationalists left the country and went into exile in Argentina,
Mexico, and Cuba. One group organized an emigré government
in Paris to await the day of liberation. Those Basques who
remained in the homeland were split by a generation gap. Older
Basques were faced with an annoying dilemma. If they condemned activism, they would be discredited in the eyes of their
fellow Basques. On the other hand, if they remained silent, they
would be regarded by Franco as traitors and pay a severe penalty
as accomplices of the extremists. Young militants, however,
were in a hurry and turned to violence. They criticized the
moderate Basque Nationalist Party (P.N.V.) as weak and ineffective and called for war against the central regime. They would
not rest until they had won independence for the four Basque
provinces in Spain and for eventual union with the three in
France. As the first generation of Basques to be free from
memories of the Civil War, they set a goal of counteracting
Franco's violence with a violence of their own. They organized a
military branch comprising 300 members for direct action and
another 300 designated for intelligence, cover, and shelter. Both
military and civilian branches were told to hold normal jobs and

to melt into the general population. Orders were followed strictly. Attached to the E.T.A. ("Basque Homeland for Liberty"), they entered wholeheartedly into the campaign of terror.

E.T.A. leaders organized their actions carefully. Because it was important to gather funds for the cause, militants were told to rob banks and extract money from industrialists. They were told to regard these raids as "revolutionary strikes" and as "revolutionary taxes," not as crimes but as necessary prerequisites for freedom. The youngest of the militants were set to work plastering walls with E.T.A. slogans, surreptitiously placing bombs in the cars of government officials, and dynamiting deserted Civil Guard posts. The campaign was similar to that of the I.R.A., in Ireland. Both the E.T.A. and the I.R.A. turned their backs on normal life in society. From their point of view, it was war against oppressors, a fight to the death for freedom and self-determination.

The activities of the E.T.A. were grim and deadly. In August 1938, E.T.A. gunmen assassinated Meliton Manzanas Gonzales, police chief of the Basque province. To them he was "the butcher of our people." This, they said, was a victory against Madrid's oppression and a warning to the authorities. An E.T.A. communiqué justified the killing. "We set up our own tribunal, condemned Gonzales to death, and executed him. Our Central Committee has decided on additional executions." For the E.T.A. this was civil war. Violence was to be met with violence. Madrid responded with mass arrests. Six E.T.A. members were arrested, quickly tried, found guilty, and condemned to death. Basque workers organized protest strikes. There were calls abroad for clemency in many countries including the Soviet Union. Franco commuted the death sentences to thirty years imprisonment.

The confrontation continued. In 1968, sixty-three government officials and policemen lost their lives in the struggle. Claiming that Franco's police were under orders not to take prisoners but to kill, E.T.A. activists struck back in kind. In December 1970 sixteen E.T.A. militants were tried by tribunal, of whom six were found guilty and sentenced to death. On January 19, 1972, four armed E.T.A. men kidnapped an industrialist near his factories in Bilbao and drove off with him in a stolen car. They announced that they would execute him as a

"Fascist bourgeois" unless he reinstated 183 Basque workers he had dismissed because they started a strike for higher wages. On September 24, 1972, four persons, including a policeman, died after an E.T.A. attack. These are only samples of the continuing strife.

THE POST-FRANCO ERA. It might be supposed that Basque militancy would be muted after the death of Franco in 1975. The dictator's iron policy was succeeded in Spain by a move toward democracy, and Basques hoped for greater recognition of their rights. Moderate concessions were not enough to appease the dissidents. If anything, E.T.A. militancy increased.

The new Spanish government decided to meet the demands of Basque separatists by adopting a policy of devolution, or more properly, appeasement. In the transition to democracy it was believed that increasing polarization between the central government and the Basque nationalists could best be handled by granting some limited concessions. By a royal decree of King Juan Carlos in mid-1977, the Basque *Generalitat* was officially recognized as a "pre-autonomy body" and given the power to assume complete control of agriculture, industry, commerce, and urban development in the Basque province. From the government's point of view this was a major concession. Many Basque citizens of moderate views were attracted by it and the implication that further grants would be forthcoming. The appeasement process also gave Basques the right to display their once forbidden red-white-and-green flag.

These concessions came, unfortunately, at a time when there was an economic downturn in the Basque economy. Wealthy Basques had left the province, investments lagged, and there was an increase in unemployment. Extremists, taking advantage of the declining economic situation, denounced Madrid's concessions as too little and too late. "Orders from Madrid," complained one militant, "sound as if they come from another planet."

Instead of accepting the government's devolution process, Basque militants began to intensify their attacks. Once again agitation clashed with police counteraction. Army officers, now losing their preferred positions under Franco, denounced the "softness" of the government and came close to mutiny. Far from settling the issue, the government's policy of concessions led to increasing polarization.

On February 23, 1978, E.T.A. militants fatally shot a federal policeman, who had stopped his car at a crossroad. On July 10, 1978, a clash between Basque demonstrators and riot police turned Pamplona into a bloody battleground, with more than 135 people injured. Basques threw bottles at the police, who responded with smoke bombs and rubber bullets. E.T.A. nationalists proclaimed a death list of government officials. On November 16, 1978, a Basque militant rode up to a judge outside of his home and killed him in revenge for his imprisonment of dissidents during the Franco regime. Members of the E.T.A. did not forget what had happened in the past. On December 6, 1976, just before there was to be a referendum on the new Spanish Constitution, three young men burst into a crowded bar in San Sebastian and killed three policemen. They left shouting: "Long live a free Basque land!"

At the same time Basque separatists continued their campaign to gather funds for their cause. It is estimated that in 1968 alone, E.T.A. militants stole an estimated $2.5 million from banks and raids on payrolls. Basque businessmen and industrialists were required to pay enormous sums to ensure their safety against E.T.A. terrorist attacks. On March 26, 1978, more than a half million Basques marched through the streets of Bilbao in the first celebration of their national day since the Spanish Civil War. There were similar demonstrations in Pamplona and other Basque cities. The marchers included nationalists and tradeunionists. There were shouts such as: "Long live an autonomous Basque country!" and "Independence now!"

In 1979, Basque militants extended their campaign to the prosperous Spanish tourist industry in the Costa del Sud. For many thousands of Europeans, including wealthy Germans, this was a favorite vacation place. Aware of its importance for the Spanish economy, E.T.A. members decided to strike at Madrid by beginning attacks on the tourist trade. An additional goal was to free a hundred comrades who had been imprisoned in Spain and have them transferred from the south to the Basque area. In addition, Basques attacked French trains moving into Spain; they wanted to force the French government to recognize captured guerrillas in French jails as "political fugitives." During

1980 the separatist campaign took some 120 lives in the bitter confrontation.

Few Basque citizens dared openly to criticize E.T.A. violence. There was an undercurrent of praise for the "liberators." The favored attitude: "We do not like E.T.A. methods, but we do admire their idealism." That the "idealism" was often extended into murder and assassination was considered beyond the point. For Basque nationalists this was a matter of life and death and they would not tolerate any opposition from their own kind. Privately, many Basques believed that violence was a necessary concomitant for their desire for freedom.

RECALCITRANT PRIESTS. The tenacity of Basque resistance may be judged by the fact that it attracted the loyal support of the lower ranks of the Roman Catholic clergy. Basques, proud of Saint Ignatius of Loyola, who was of Basque origin and who had exhibited the kind of independence the Basques held dear, were most loyal Catholics. For them the village was regarded as the traditional stronghold of their culture and values. The upper church hierarchy, largely conservative, objected to E.T.A. violence and especially opposed its championing of the class struggle. Bishops supported a policy of moderation as well as cooperation with the centralized authorities.

The views of the regular clergy (monks) and secular clergy (priests) were similar. In a church known for its discipline and obedience, Basque priests and monks tended to oppose their own hierarchy. There was a sensational turn in ecclesiastical matters when many of the lower clergy turned to extremism in the confrontation between Basque separatists and the centralized government. A young priest said: "One can be a Christian and still work with the E.T.A." Another stated: "Violence is imposed upon us. We have no other recourse because the Franco regime has made dialogue and negotiation impossible." E.T.A. separatists in trouble found sympathy and support among young priests. In mid-May 1979 a taxi driver was murdered outside Bilbao after police raided an E.T.A. meeting. The next morning two priests bound up the bullet wounds of a man they found unconscious in a nearby village. The police arrested eight priests, who were sent to prison at Zamora, where there was a special wing for confining priests and monks.

The "bandit priests" of the Basque province opposed the Franco regime as dictatorial and anti-humanitarian. Franco regarded them as dangerous traitors. He ordered the arrest of those priests who said mass for E.T.A. guerrillas killed by the police. His Civil Guards raided monasteries in the Basque province, confiscated banned books, searched for Basque flags, and subjected clerical prisoners to interrogation. Priests were charged with "insulting the armed forces," considered to be a serious matter in Franco's Spain. In Rome, the papacy made only feeble efforts at mediation. It saw Franco as its loyal protector and was reluctant to interfere in what it regarded as local problems. The practice of harassing Basque priests ceased after the death of Franco in 1975, when the dictatorship was ended and the trend toward a democratic regime began.

THE BASQUES OF FRANCE. Although there were twin separatist movements by Basques in both Spain and France, the two dissenting ethnic groups never quite achieved the harmony they desired. Yet, the history of the Basques is associated with that of both Spain and France. Spanish and French Basques resisted inroads by Visigoths, Franks, Normans, and Moors. The two *Euskera*-speaking regions on either side of the border never formed a single political system. There were, instead, social and cultural relationships expressed in similar rural customs. Each of the three French provinces, Labourd, Basse-Navarre, and Soule, had its own judicial structure before being absorbed by the French state. The French government, strongly opposed to regional autonomy, combined the three provinces into the large southwestern *département* of Basse-Pyrenees. Throughout the nineteenth century the French authorities tightened their hold on the Basques. Holding rigid control, they regarded the Basques as a backward conglomeration of farmers, seafarers, and smugglers. Across the border the Basques were to play a prominent role in Spanish affairs, while their kinsmen on the other side of the Pyrenees remained inconspicuous in French life.

At the end of the nineteenth century, Basque resentment against control from Paris began to appear. But it was not until the 1930s that there were increasing calls for regional autonomy. Basque dissenters in France began to speak of their brotherhood with the Basques of Spain. As in Spain, French Basques began to call for unity of the three French provinces as well as a confederation with the four Basque provinces in Spain. They accused the French government of giving them little attention and of thrusting them into a low place in French society.

In the two decades after 1950, French Basques, stimulated by the extremist activities of Basques across the border, began to increase their activities for autonomy. They received support from Spanish Basque extremists but otherwise there was little interest from moderate Basques in Spain.

The attitude of Paris to Basque separatists was precisely the same as its judgment of Breton nationalism. To French authorities this was "subversion" and treason, activities not to be allowed in the centralized French state. French police in 1979 made a series of early morning raids on homes of Basque sympathizers, arresting twenty-three and expelling to Spain seven members of the Basque guerrillas. An official communiqué stated that Spanish Basques would no longer be allowed on French soil. Public opinion throughout France supported this attitude. French nationalism would brook no competing nationalisms.

NATIONALISMS IN CONFRONTATION. The struggle between Spain's centralized nationalism and Basque separatist nationalism indicates that not every nation-state in the contemporary world has been able to maintain its authority over a recalcitrant minority. It is the usual clash between two kinds of nationalism, one of which seeks to maintain unity of disparate elements, and the other which is disruptive and wants a national existence of its own. How to reconcile these two goals has become a major problem in the era of nation-states. The upsurge of mini-nationalisms, accompanied by violence, makes it most difficult to maintain the peace so ardently desired by people all over the world.

CHAPTER 9

CANADIAN DILEMMA:
FRANCOPHONES VERSUS ANGLOPHONES

DE GAULLE'S JUDGMENT. In July 1967 the French President Charles de Gaulle, nationalist *par excellence*, journeyed to Canada on an official visit. After a triumphant tour through French Canada he arrived in Montreal to an enthusiastic reception. He spoke from the balcony of the City Hall in his familiar sepulchral tone. At the end of his talk, he suddenly shouted the slogan: "*Vive le Québec libre!*" ("Long live free Quebec!").

It was an astonishing and totally unexpected performance. De Gaulle, one of the great egoists of the twentieth century, was known throughout the world as a dedicated apostle of French nationalism. He believed that he not only spoke for France, he was France. His mind was filled with battle pictures in which his beloved compatriots were always winning. France, he believed, had an exalted destiny and the nation could not exist without greatness. In World War II, Allied leaders had to contend with de Gaulle's stiffness and arrogance. Churchill saw him as an annoying problem, Roosevelt dismissed him as a latter-day Joan of Arc.

It may be that de Gaulle considered his slogan merely as a reminder to the Quebecers fellow Frenchmen at home that the two were united as cousins in a special cultural association. He, himself, may have seen his catch phrase merely as a compliment to a French-speaking community in the industrial world. On the other hand, it might well have been calculated support for rising French separatism in Canada.

Quebec separatists were simply delighted. For them this was a slogan of enormous import. In their minds it meant help for their cause by one of the world's great statesmen. They saw the event as a significant step in their aim to reverse Britain's conquest of French Canada.

Anglophones in Canada were not amused by de Gaulle's

controversial declaration. For them it was a blunder of the first magnitude, as well as unwarranted interference in Canadian affairs. Authorities informed him that his statement was unacceptable and that he was no longer welcome in Canada. English Canadians regarded their country as not a British or French idea, but as a confederation of English and French ethnic groups. They saw the progress and accomplishments of their country as due to the joint efforts of both peoples. They urged the visiting French President to keep his nose out of Canadian affairs.

The incident brought to global attention the mounting differences between Anglophones and Francophones in Canada. The country was in an uncomfortable quandary about the conflict between the two peoples. Here, again, was a serious confrontation between a centralized nationalism and the separatist nationalism of a dissenting minority. The problem was not limited to Canada. Throughout the world there were similar manifestations of rivalry between the two kinds of nationalism, between the power of the centralized state and those dissidents who demanded self-determination and sovereignty for themselves.

THE ETHNIC MÉLANGE. From its early history Canada developed in the condition of a state composed of two disparate elements. The desired assimilation of linguistic Anglophones and Francophones has never been achieved. Instead, a rivalry has emerged that continues to the present day. In addition to linguistic and cultural differences there are political, economic, and psychological variants that have kept the two peoples apart. The French-speaking people who settled in Quebec look to French traditions, while the English-speaking citizens pay attention to their English heritage. Both groups have differing ideas on the nature of the nation. Anglophones hope for a single federal state comprising one nation, with two languages, two cultures, and a combined future. Francophones lean to the idea of two sovereign states, one French-speaking and settled in Quebec and the other English-speaking with the capital at Ottawa.

In its early history, the rich Canadian territory was fought for by both British and French. Eventually, the two peoples were combined in a federal union that was not altogether stable from the start. Canada became less of a nation than a combination of regional population pockets scattered over large areas. The relationship of Canada to Great Britain was always a complicated matter. The British North American Act (1867) was the country's founding document. Important powers were reserved for the British Parliament. One of its passages referred to the division of powers between the centralized federal government and the provinces. The latter never quite agreed on a formula that would remove all colonial ties with Britain. The constitutional situation led to much dissatisfaction throughout Canada, but especially in the province of Quebec with its French background and its reluctance to submit to Anglophone control. Quebecers did not feel that they were assigned an equal place in the confederation. Many of them believed that they were subjugated to foreigners. They turned to their own idea of nationalism. The result was confrontation that has existed to the present day.

ROOTS OF DISSENSION. The history of Canada is a story of intense rivalry between British and French for control of the vast territory. Where in the United States the country emerged as a "melting pot" of varied peoples, Canada remained divided. Actually, Canada was one country composed of two major groups, English and French. From the beginning there were linguistic, cultural, and psychological differences between the two peoples. In addition, there were divergent religions. The majority of the English hewed to Protestantism, the French were Roman Catholic. How to reconcile the distinguishing characteristics of Anglophones and Francophones became a problem of the first magnitude. Each side developed its own idea of nationalism. The matter entered a critical phase when one group managed to seize control over the other.

Both English and French claimed priority in the matter of who got to Canada first. In 1497 and 1498, Italian explorers John Cabot and Sebastian Cabot, working for the English, reached Labrador. In 1534, French explorer Jacques Cartier landed on the Gaspé Peninsula, sailed to the Gulf of St. Lawrence, reached Quebec in 1535, and began fur trading in the area. Samuel de Champlain established the first French settlement in Canada in 1608. Frenchmen who resided in Quebec were attracted by the

riches of the interior territory. New France had its French view
of life, which emphasized the feudal system transplanted from
Europe. The Roman Catholic Church assumed a powerful
position in the area.

The English, too, were allured by the riches of the Canadian
territory. They regarded the discoveries of the Cabots as giving
them priority in the area. The French penetrated into the
interior, while the British settled mainly in the coastal region. In
this early stage, each side regarded the other as an interloper.
The rivalry between the English and French on the European
scene was extended to the New World. The European Seven
Years' War (1756–1763) was also fought in North America,
where it was known as the French and Indian Wars. The
differences between English and French in Canada eventually
led to war. In 1759 British General James Wolfe defeated French
General Louis de Montcalm on the Plains of Abraham. The
Treaty of Paris in 1763 brought an end to New France and
established British rule in Canada. In Europe the French were so
weakened by their campaign against Frederick the Great that
they could not maintain their widely separated forts in Canada.

For the next century Canada was part of British North
America. British officials faced a critical problem of how to deal
with a proud people of French background who felt that they had
been robbed of their territory. The Quebec Act of 1774 was
designed to stabilize British rule by recognizing French rights in
language, religion, and civil law. This was the beginning of a
long process of appeasement that never seemed to be successful. Anglo-French rivalry in Canada led to Francophone rebel-
lions in 1837. London sent Lord Durham to win back disaffected
Francophones in Canada. His *Report* (1839) became the Magna
Carta of the British colonial system.

On July 1, 1867, came the great landmark of Canadian history
with the British North America Act (B.N.A.). The French
language was given equal status with English in the Parliament
at Ottawa, in the Quebec legislature, and in the federal law
courts. From 1867 to 1914 Canada extended its course of nation-
building. In 1931 the Statute of Westminster established equality
of the Canadian Parliament with that of Britain.

There was increasing dissatisfaction in French Canada. Francophones, always uncomfortable under British domination, re-

jected British efforts at accommodation. They especially resented a foreign policy which they regarded as too imperialistic
in design. Quebec, they insisted, was the homeland of a distinct
people with a separate language, culture, institutions, traditions, and economic resources. This attitude crystallized into a
demand by separatists for sovereignty and independence. Canada, like many other countries, was afflicted by a clash of
nationalisms.

LANGUAGE, CULTURE, AND ECONOMICS. Three
main elements contribute to the differences between Francophones and Anglophones. First, language, a powerful factor
in the structural composition of nationalism, was of special
importance in the confrontation. Like the natives of France.
Quebecers take pride in their language. They regard French as a
superior linguistic possession and defend it enthusiastically.
English authorities recognized this special affinity for linguistic
identity and over the course of decades made many concessions
for its use in schools and legal affairs.

The population of Canada (1989 est.) is 25,344,000. Those
from the British Isles number 47 percent, the French 27 percent,
and other Europeans 23 percent. In Quebec the French-
speaking majority runs to 80 percent. It claims to be a French
island in an English sea. Quebecers argue that their language
forms the main ingredient of a nation-state. "More and more,"
they say, "in Quebec it is in French that things are happening."
They see their language as appropriate to self-government and
claim that any national group of substance deserves to govern
itself. (*See Reading No. 37.*)

In August 1978 the long-standing bilingual clash was intensified when the Quebec authorities made an attempt to preserve
French by restricting the use of English. A Draconian law,
known as Bill 101, made French the only "official" language in
Quebec. French was to be spoken in the courts and only the
French version of a legal judgment was to be regarded as
legitimate. All governmental business was to be conducted in
French. Doctors and lawyers, as a condition of their practice,
were to show "appropriate fluency" in French. Camille Layrin,
then Quebec's Minister of Cultural Affairs, stated bluntly that
Bill 101 was designed to make Quebec "as much French as

Ottawa is English." The Quebec government was adamant: it would not settle "for a few words of French." The Association of English-speaking School Boards announced its strong opposition to Bill 101. Quebec authorities persisted and decreed that all posters and signboards were to be in French. The issue of language continued to become a major source of friction between the two peoples.

The language problem reflected the cultural differences between Anglophones and Francophones. There was little cross-fertilization and no fusing or melting of diverse strains. Largely derivative, Canadian culture reflected its British counterpart. Canadian writers—novelists, poets, dramatists, and historians, looked to London for inspiration. The nationalist emphasis was diffuse and subtle, but it was English culture which played a dominating role in Canadian affairs. French-Canadian literary activity in the middle of the nineteenth century revealed the rise of Quebec's nationalism. French writers showed a sense of pride in their past and a determination to protect their heritage. Richard Jones described the sentiment: "The French Canadian of our day considers himself, consciously or unconsciously, to be a part of a colonized minority. It is this particular image that is the source of his nationalism."

Many French writers asserted the uniqueness of their culture in Quebec. Gaston Miron, who developed a reputation as the voice of Quebec nationalism, urged his fellow citizens to unite for the cause of separatism. "The majority of our creators," he said, "the novelists, playwrights, artists, poets, and singers, are in favor of independence as well as a strong portion of the intelligentsia, the scholars, and the university people." He was certain: the trend to independence, in his view, was "irreversible."

The efforts to build a bridge between the two cultures had to face thorny difficulties. McGill University in Montreal, regarded as a symbol of Canada's Anglophone elite, had to face an increasingly assertive French-speaking student body. On one occasion, thousands of French-speaking students marched on the campus and shouted such slogans as "*McGill Française!*" The provincial government, responsible for a major portion of the university's budget, retaliated by beginning a fiscal squeeze.

The cultural conflict did not mesh well with the Anglophone goal of unity in diversity.

Added to linguistic and cultural differences were economic grievances by the Francophones in Quebec. Citizens of Quebec felt that they were unfairly shut out of Canada's economic life. Canada was rich in natural resources and, despite its considerable distances and harsh climate, had developed into a prosperous industrialized state. French Canadians believed that they were not assigned a proper role in this economic development. They saw themselves as condemned to a second-rate part in the economic development of Canada. They were not satisfied with their subsidiary place in a federal union in which they were supposed to have equal rights. Wanting a greater share of Canada's riches, they demanded more economic security.

Quebec's nationalists complained that they had resources, business, and industry of their own, including global markets. However, they believed that they had been shut out from a proper function in a dual society. They demanded a greater share in business and industry and complained that they were relegated to a position as "hewers of wood and drawers of water." They were victims, they said, of "a poisonous climate maintained in great part by the English-speaking media and by federal propaganda." They had been condemned, they claimed, to a low status in Canadian society and they would not cease to agitate for separation as an independent national state. It was the familiar cry of nationalists who felt that they possessed all the attributes of a nation-state but were held in bondage.

REFORMISTS AND TERRORISTS. Quebec's nationalists in the 1950s expressed their opposition to what they called "federal authoritarianism." The Quebec Liberal Party, with a platform dedicated to reform, came to power in 1961. It inaugurated what it called "the Quiet Revolution," designed to modernize the province and give preference to French culture. The central government in Ottawa, concerned about this trend, offered special status to Quebec: it would not be required to participate in the federal welfare program. Anglophones denounced the concession as appeasement. Francophone extremists reacted with a series of bombings in the English-speaking district of Montreal. In July 1963 Prime Minister Lester Bowles Pearson appointed a Bilingual and Bicultural Commission, consisting of five Francophones and five Anglophones, to recommend what should be done "to develop the Canadian Confederation on the basis of equal partnership between the two founding races."

The Commission stated that Canada, without being fully conscious of the fact, was passing through the greatest crisis in its history. Its final report (1967) proposed to establish nationwide equality in languages at both federal and provincial levels. Dissatisfied Quebec extremists kidnapped James Cross, British Trade Commissioner in Montreal. They abducted and murdered Pierre Laport, Quebec's Labor Minister. Prime Minister Pierre Trudeau invoked Canada's 1914 War Measures Act and placed the country under martial law. Meanwhile, separatist leaders condemned "this sick confederation" and presented the slogan "Quebec for Québécois!" They insisted that there was no satisfactory coexistence and only a continuous aggression by the majority.

Most Quebecers were moderates who hoped to see the problem solved without violence. A small extremist group, the *Front Libération de Québec* (F.L.Q.), launched a program of bombing, burning, and looting. At first it used mild devices, but in 1967 its members set off a powerful detonation at the Montreal Stock Exchange, which caused twenty-seven injuries. By the fall of 1970 the F.L.Q. had claimed six lives.

TRUDEAU AND LÉVESQUE. The problem of federalism versus separation became the central issue of Canadian and Quebecian politics. Two figures were to play important roles in this confrontation: Prime Minister Pierre Trudeau and Quebec's Premier René Lévesque. Both were to take opposed positions on the issue as long as they remained in office.

Pierre Trudeau, debonair, fluently bilingual, was born in Montreal, but he became the champion of national unity. He was Canadian Prime Minister in 1968. He stated two goals: "One was to make sure that Quebec would not leave Canada through separation and the other was to make sure that Canada would not shove Quebec out through narrow-mindedness." He believed that Quebecers must be masters in their own house, but it was essential that the house be the whole of Canada. He was adamant: "Most Canadians understand that the rupture of their country would be a crime against the history of mankind." He saw it as a disaster for the rest of Canada.

René Lévesque, described as a "chain-smoking, disorganized, hot tempered bundle of emotional energy," was a fervent Quebec nationalist. He became Premier of Quebec in 1976. He believed in separation, but insisted that it be implemented "in a positive way," peacefully and in a democratic manner. The Confederation, he said, "has been a negative force and only force of habit has held Quebec to it. We are like two trains going farther and farther away from each other. For thirty years Quebec has been moving towards self-affirmation, self-determination, and self-government, which does not mesh with the federal system." Lévesque died on November 1, 1987. At that time there was a revival of Quebec nationalism.

REFERENDUM: THE HISTORIC TEST. The issue was put to a historic test on May 20, 1980, when a referendum was held on the matter of Quebec's sovereignty. (*See Reading No. 38.*) The turnout was one of the heaviest in Quebec's electoral history. Those Quebecers in the polling booth apparently had second thoughts when voting. In a stunning vote, the citizens of Quebec rejected the move to sovereignty. The "No" vote was 2,140,815 or 59.4 percent, the "Yes" vote was 1,475,509, or 40.6 percent. The separatists did not even win a majority of the Francophones, who made up 80 percent of the population of the province. Some 54 percent of the French-speaking Quebecers joined with more than 80 percent of the Anglophone minority to produce a federalist victory.

Jubilant federalists cheered their victory. Young militants in East Montreal demonstrated and shouted "We want a country!" Lévesque conceded defeat but urged his followers to fight "until next time."

Despite the referendum, the issue of separation has not been stifled in Canada. National unity is still at stake in the continuing power struggle. An all-out Canadian consensus remains difficult in the presence of a highly emotional, persistent demand for self-determination. Here, as elsewhere in the world, the confrontation between two kinds of nationalism remains alive and unsettled.

The situation in Canada reveals the upward surge of nationalism. In one form or another nationalism exists everywhere in world society. It retains its tenacious hold in nation-states, whether advanced or backward. Canada may be included among the progressive nations, but like smaller and weaker states it is subject to the dangers of dissatisfied ethnic nationalism.

CHAPTER 10

CONCLUSIONS AND SUMMARY

BLESSING OR CURSE. In 1926 Columbia University's Carlton J. H. Hayes prepared the way for the study of nationalism by treating two sides of the historical phenomenon. Nationalism, in his view, could be either blessing or curse. On the one hand, it is a desirable element when used to describe "wholesome national patriotism," and represents a community with similar characteristics such as language, customs, and historical traditions. Hayes conceded that there might be a "sweet, amiable nationalism which will bring forth a good fruit in abundance and will be to all men a solace and a blessing." This was the type of nationalism that in its early stage as advocated by Herder was a blessing for mankind. According to Herder, the human race is a unit in which all nations should dwell in harmony for "the cultivation of humanity."

On the other hand, Hayes saw that over the course of the nineteenth century nationalism was transformed radically into an evil stage—an integral form. There merged a new trinity—the combination of nationality, the national state, and national patriotism. These became the source of grave abuses. In its new form nationalism was permeated with a spirit of exclusiveness and narrowness that fed on inordinate pride in one's identity and on gross ignorance of others. This was the sort of nationalism that contributed much to the outbreak of two World Wars and the slaughter of millions of human beings. (*See Reading No. 39.*)

The Hayes formula influenced generations of scholars of nationalism, who accept his view on the historical phenomenon as blessing or curse. Boyd C. Shafer, once a colleague of Hayes, commented on the blessings of nationalism. For human beings all over the world, nationalism brought hopes, even if illusory, for a better, fuller, freer life, for a safer order, and it gave patriots the opportunity to feel glory, splendor, and pride. Unfortunately, this attractive side would be replaced. National pride turned out to be unreal, deceptive, and misleading. To build the nation-state and maintain it against all dangers became the goal of society. Group solidarities were opposed to other solidarities in so vehement a fashion that nationalism was transformed into a curse. (*See Reading No. 40.*)

NATIONALISM PERSISTENT. Despite the tragic record of two World Wars in the twentieth century, nationalism retained its power as a historical force in the contemporary world. People still regard the status of a nation-state as of overwhelming importance. They derive great satisfaction from the belief that they are members of a superior nation. Not only that, they see their strength in group cohesion. They feel that they must not reject the sense of belonging in favor of a questionable belief in a harmonious world. They see their nation as chosen by God or fate to fulfill an exalted mission in the world.

British journalist Barbara Ward saw the staying power of nationalism as linked closely with the problem of power in contemporary society. In our world, she said, the final power is exercised by the nation-state, whether by force under a despotic government, or by general consent under a democratic government. Any kind of government is based on its ability to impose its policies and achieve its will. This means that absolute sovereignty is exercised by the state alone. Hence, the nation-state becomes the most important point in all our problems. The nation-state, or nationalism, becomes the focal point of existence. Nationalism remains strong because it is a manifestation of the Western search for freedom under law. (*See Reading No. 41.*)

It is true that for a decade or so after World War I there was a temporary retreat from nationalism. The feeling was widespread that nationalism was no longer the dominant political philosophy of the day. It soon became evident that nationalism had a lot of life in it. The sentiment of absolute loyalty to the nation-state was revived and nationalism appeared again in its evil form. The nationalist concept had been developing since the close of World War I, when the League of Nations revealed its inability to solve the differences among nation-states. The United Nations after World War II was similarly afflicted with preference for the nation-state in human affairs. Nations had little desire for lessening the power of their sovereignty. (*See Reading No. 42.*)

By no means has the staying power of nationalism brought greater peace and security. Quite to the contrary, it has led to new conflicts and exacerbated new tensions. Elie Kedourie, British scholar of nationalism, believes that the nation-states which inherited the position of the empires were not an improvement. "They did not minister to political freedom, they did not increase prosperity, and their existence was not conducive to peace. In fact, the national question which their setting up, it was hoped, would solve, became, on the contrary, more bitter and envenomed." *(See Reading No. 43.)*

EUROCRATS AND NATIONALISM. During the temporary lull in nationalism after the slaughter of World War I, one man, Richard N. Coudenhove-Kalergi, began a personal crusade to change the nation-states of Europe into a federation. He denounced nationalism as a dangerous historical phenomenon and insisted that cooperation should be the goal of all civilized human beings. There could be no united world, he said, without a united Europe. In his opinion, what was needed was a federated Europe on the model of the United States and Switzerland. To achieve that goal he devoted his entire career to promotion of the idea of a Pan-Europa. As early as 1922 he presented the first draft of his project. He sought the help of distinguished statesmen, who assured him of their support but refused to head the movement. He published a long series of books on Pan-Europa and headed a series of Pan-European Congresses. He never ceased his passionate proposal of European unity.

Coudenhove-Kalergi's crusade had an underlying weakness: it had no mass base. Some like-minded intellectuals gave him their attention and support, but the general public was uninterested. To most people the zealous advocate of a united Europe was an ineffectual crusader who misunderstood the reality of the nation-state.

Yet, the movement for a United States of Europe did not die. In the 1950s it received the support of two French officials, Robert Schuman and Jean Monnet. Both favored a community based on the equality of rights of each confederated state under a common authority and discipline. A European community would open up hitherto unsuspected perspectives. Europe has a "noble primacy." It was not merely a continental but a global necessity. Europe must strengthen herself inwardly, not in her own interest but for the sake of humanity. Both Schuman and Monnet were gradualists who advocated a step-by-step process leading to continental unity. A fragmented Europe, they believed, would always be burdened by wars. In their view the nation-state was drawing to a close and the days of national sovereignty were ended. Sovereignty, they said, must be transferred eventually into a consolidated, harmonious United States of Europe.

According to Schuman and Monnet, the first phase of a new Europe must be economic. Schuman declared: "The pooling of the production of coal and steel will immediately establish a common basis for economic development." Thus will be realized, simply and rapidly, the fusion of interests which will be indispensable for the establishment of an economic community between countries long opposed by bloody conflict. This will set up the basis for a European confederation indispensable for the safeguarding of peace. On March 25, 1957, the Treaty of Rome established the European Economic Community.

For Eurocrats the Common Market was merely the first step on the road to political integration. On June 7, 1979, and on three succeeding days, 175 million people of the European Community voted in an election for the European Parliament. Since then the movement has gathered momentum as Eurocrats boast of the shaping of a "New Europe." (*See Reading No. 44.*)

Many critics, geared to the old nationalism, reject the Eurocrats as impractical idealists who do not understand the nature of the modern nation-state. No statesman, they argue, could take upon himself the burden of supporting an idea that could diminish the sovereignty of his homeland—that would be close to treason. They say that officials of contemporary Europe may seem to support the idea of political unity, but they draw the line at any hint of transferring political sovereignty to a European body. This view was expressed by both Charles de Gaulle and Margaret Thatcher, both of whom stubbornly put their nation above all else.

Critics point out that from its beginning the European Parliament has been faced with the problem of its relations with national parliaments. The balance between national and supranational elements in the Community's constitutional structure is unclear and uncertain. An aggravating question remains: would the future European union be no more than another intergovernmental organization, or was the European Community indeed developing into a new form of political-economic association? The question remains unsolved. Thus far, say the critics, the European Parliament is an ephemeral institution with very little power. There is no mass movement calling for transfer of sovereignty from the national to the European level. Critics of the Eurocrats maintain that the peoples of European states continue to think of themselves as citizens of their *national* state and do not relish the idea of European citizenship in the contemporary world.

SOVIET ETHNONATIONALISMS. Jonas Salk, developer of the anti-polio vaccine, saw significance in the fact that things come in pairs: matter-energy, positive-negative, male-female, intuition-reason. In his view this is a dynamic, interactively symmetric relationship. It applies not only to biology but also to political relationships including nationalism. In its development nationalism has been both a force for union and a force for disruption. In many countries there exists a clash between the unifying force of a centralized nationalism and the dissenting movements of ethnic groups demanding self-determination, freedom, and sovereignty.

The Soviet Union revealed an excellent example of the confrontation between the two kinds of nationalism. The Bolsheviks emerged in 1917 to seize power and begin the great experiment in communism. Karl Marx presented a new ideology: scientific socialism would make for a better world than capitalism; nationalism would disappear as a force in world affairs. The Bolsheviks smashed the old Russian Empire and killed Czar Nicholas II and his family. Lenin went ahead to create a new society "rid of the grotesque evils of capitalism." The "dictatorship of the proletariat" (read "dictatorship of the Communist Party") was created to control the wave of the future.

During seven decades the Soviet Union went on to achieve the reputation of a Great Superpower. It constructed a hugh military edifice to protect itself against "jealous" capitalist nations. The masses were held in line by a huge propaganda machine hammering away at what it conceived to be the "truth." Those who objected in any way were subjected to the terror of a long line of secret police. Eventually, the U.S.S.R. appeared before the world as an innovator in space exploration and as a nation possessing many nuclear weapons. As for rivalry with the capitalist world, Nikita Khruschchev issued his confident judgment: "We will bury you!"

Over the decades, however, it became increasingly obvious that there were major flaws in Communist ideology and in communism in action. Marxist "scientific socialism" turned out to be a false conception. Equally wrong was the contention that Soviet nationalities would disappear in a highly centralized national state. While the Soviet system was presented to the world as a kind of paradise, inside its borders communism was just not working. Public conditions went from bad to worse. The problems of production and consumption went unsolved. Standing in line for hours to seek necessities became a way of life. Wheat, the essential for bread, lay rotting in the fields: the Kremlin was forced to buy it from its "decadent" capitalist enemies. Meat, cigarettes, vodka, toothpaste began to disappear from the shelves of businesses. Meanwhile, Communist Party members appropriated the available apartments, dachas in the countryside, and automobiles.

By the mid-1980s the situation approached chaos. Little had been done to control the epidemic of empty shelves. Out of the maelstrom of a nation in great trouble appeared Mikhail S. Gorbachev. To rescue his troubled country, he introduced a series of reforms. He proclaimed *glasnost* (openness) and *perestroika* (restructuring). More, he even hinted at the acceptance of such capitalist devices as competition and a market economy. His problems were increased enormously by what was happening in the constituent republics. In 1989, starting in the Baltic states, one after another of the fifteen republics began to demand self-determination, sovereignty, independence. Everywhere Communist parties were thrown out of power. Added to the Kremlin's troubles was the falling apart of its satellites, which had been constructed carefully as barrier states against the West. The Berlin Wall was breached and Gorbachev gave his assent to the reunification of Germany. The Soviet Union was in a precarious state as its unity was besieged by demanding ethnonationalisms.

The issue came to a head in late August 1991, when the expected backlash from the right came with tanks rolling into central Moscow. The attempted coup lasted just three days as enraged citizens throughout the country, casting aside their fears, smashed the ill-organized attempt to renew the dictatorship. The calls for democracy and a market economy were too loud to be stilled.

GERMANY AND NATIONALISM. Germany in the first 45 years of the twentieth century underwent a devastating experience with the wrong kind of nationalism. The blustering nationalism of Kaiser Wilhelm II calling for "a place in the sun" and the aggressive nationalism of Adolf Hitler brought Germans into the abyss of two World Wars with tragic consequences. In 1945 the country was in a desperate condition, its cities smashed into ruins, its young manhood sacrificed to satisfy the ambitions of an unstable dictator.

After 1945, slowly but surely, the German people recovered from the effects of nationalism gone berserk. The nationalism and militarism that had been their stock-in-trade in the past vanished and were cast into the dustbins of history. Accepting a new democracy, they turned their backs on their past history and devoted their many talents to the construction of a prosperous state. What happened has been termed "an economic miracle." A stable democracy emerged from the ruins. The government admitted the sins of the past and vowed that never again would it ruin its reputation by dangerous forays into aggressive nationalism. The New Germany gained the respect even of those peoples who had been victims of Nazi barbarism.

The reunification of the two Germanies in 1990 brought the country into the front of European affairs. Some observers, influenced by German conduct in the past, expressed alarm. In their view it was possible that Germany might return to the ways of the old nationalism. The leaders of reunited Germany hastened to explain that they had no wish to dominate Europe. On the contrary, they proclaimed themselves as Europeans, not as an isolated nationalist country. They supported a Charter for a New Europe. They expressed agreement with the novelist Thomas Mann, who had called for "not a German Europe but a European Germany." They opted for patriotism as love of country, and cast aside the kind of nationalism that had distinguished their government in the past.

Most of all, the Germans underwent a major change in their national character. For them the older characteristics of obedience, militancy, and arrogance were outworn relics and were rejected. A new, healthy democracy had emerged. Contemporary Germans accept a humanitarian nationalism far removed from the relics of the past.

ETHNICITY IN YUGOSLAVIA. The examples treated in this study are selected among the many existing all over the world. It would take volumes to consider similar outbreaks of nationalism everywhere. The conglomerate state of Yugoslavia presents a prime illustration of how nationalism can work as a disintegrative force in human affairs. The attachments of language, region, and religion persist. These are not preindustrial remnants about to disappear in modern society. Peoples of widely divergent views do not combine peacefully in one unified national state. Yugoslavia, in the midst of the unstable Balkans, was composed of ethnic nationalists who preferred conflict to living together in a harmonious society.

In 1914 only Serbia and Montenegro were independent states in the area, while Croatia, Slovenia, and Bosnia and Hercegovina formed part of the Austro-Hungarian Empire. In 1945 the monarchy was abolished and the Yugoslav People's Republic was established by Josip Broz, called Tito. His victorious Communist Partisans seized control at the end of World War II. Under his strong leadership the divided ethnic factions were kept together in an uneasy relationship. In 1946 the federation of six republics was expelled from the Cominform after Tito resisted attempts by Stalin to dominate his regime. Tito opted for "national communism."

After Tito's death in 1980 Yugoslavia plunged into difficulties as the ethnic groups turned on one another. Internal tensions multiplied. Political rivalry increased between Serbia, the largest of the six republics, and Slovenia and Croatia, the most prosperous of the Yugoslav states. Added to this problem was the repression by Serbia of its Albanian rivals in Kosovo. Stirring nationalist passions in Serbia revealed only one of the rivalries in a country weakened by dissension. Narrow nationalism threatened the very existence of the country.

Croatia and Slovenia held democratic elections which threw out Communist rule. When Serbia imposed tariffs on the goods of Croatia and Slovenia, they replied in kind. Bosnia and Hercegovina, with a mixed population of Serbs, Croats, and Muslims, attracted the attention of neighboring Serbs and Croats. Yugoslavia's Prime Minister Ante Markovic, called desperately for reform to satisfy the warring factions: "Only an undivided Yugoslavia, with a market economy, political pluralism, democratic rights and freedom for all citizens will open the door to Europe and its integration processes."

There was skeptical gloom as to the possibility of the divergent ethnic groups in Yugoslavia remaining together. Some observers predicted a breakup, accompanied by ethnic violence, even civil war. (*See Reading No. 45.*) That prediction came true in the late summer of 1991 when the situation degenerated into civil war between the Serbian army and Croatian dissidents. It was a bloody conflict as nationalism replaced centralism as Yugoslavia's creed.

OBSTREPEROUS BASQUES. Unlike Scottish or Welsh mini-nationalisms, there was little that was moderate about Basque separatism. Generations of Basques in the north of Spain regarded themselves as victims of a foreign government on their soil. They reject moderation as totally unacceptable and they turn to violence and extremism to win the self-determination they desire. They see themselves as having all the qualities of nationhood and they resent interference by Madrid in their affairs. The Basques have been stubborn in their resoluteness and tenacity and they are resistant to efforts at appeasement to lessen their demand for independence.

The struggle has been long and continuous. For the centralized nationalism of the Spanish state, Basque separatism has been one of its most pressing problems. Dictator Francisco Franco, using iron tactics, managed to hold the Basques under control, but after his death on November 20, 1975, the Basques turned again to agitation for their cause. In January 1980, following overwhelming approval in a home-rule referendum, Basques were granted a measure of autonomy. This was not at all acceptable to extremists, who saw a vast difference between autonomy and independence. They renewed their violent campaign in favor of separation.

The tradition of violence was long-standing in Basque history. Militants concentrated mainly on acts of public sabotage. Repression during the Franco regime was especially harsh. Scores of nationalists were arrested and prosecuted. Basque nationalists accused of terrorism were tried before military tribunals. This kind of regionalist rebellion during the final years of the Franco regime poses a severe problem for the unity of the Spanish state. Basque dissidence continues in contemporary Spain.

THE CANADIAN QUANDARY. The clash of cultures in Canada provides still another example of dissatisfied nationalism. The ethnic mélange proved to be an important factor in Canadian history. As elsewhere, a special problem of long-standing duration had been the relationship of the provinces to the central government. From its early history, control of the country wavered between English and French settlers. Britain's North America Act of 1867 was Canada's constitution. How to revise it to satisfy the major ethnic groups has been the subject of a long-term investigation. The French-Canadians, especially in Quebec, have turned to nationalism and have adhered rigidly to French traditions and culture. They reveal a growing demand for greater autonomy. This attitude posed a problem for Anglophones, who found it most difficult to face the nationalist demands of Quebecers.

While many French-Canadians have been attracted by extreme nationalism, they do not see the issue as intensified to a danger point. Quebecers calmly accept the polemics of separatists, but they are not attracted by the kind of terrorism supported by Basques in Spain or by Yugoslav factions. They do not relish the ways of extreme chauvinism. They see themselves as a decent people devoted to the task of holding together a national state composed of peoples of a different culture. The idea of separatism in Quebec has split the middle class and the labor unions, but those separatists who demand action for self-determination have not been able to acquire the desired unanimity of opinion. The political referendum held on May 20, 1980, rejected the move toward sovereignty. This indicated the decline of separatism as a political choice, but it did not mean the end of the conflict. The confrontation remains serious as extremist calls for separatism continue.

SURGE OF NATIONALISM. Despite its inconsistencies and paradoxes (*See Reading No. 46.*), nationalism retains its role as an extraordinarily powerful factor on the contemporary scene. It is the dominant political passion of our time. It has become more important than class or ideology. It has triumphed over those totalitarian systems that are based on class-conscious inter-nationalism. Everywhere, small ethnic groups, displaying a form of nationalism of their own, gain new momentum in their opposition to the larger nationalism of the centralized state.

In its modern form nationalism originated on the European continent in the late eighteenth century. Following the horrible slaughter of World War I, it was extended throughout the world. The war itself was a product of conflicting nationalisms. The empires of Austria-Hungary and Turkey were destroyed and in their place new national states were created. The situation was not changed by the added tragedy of World War II. Once again, new national states emerged with little attention to their ethnic composition. National rivalries were accentuated by this failure to comprehend the nature of ethnicity.

Nationalism became a global phenomenon. Peoples see their security in flag and anthem. They attach themselves to the idea of belonging. They regard their history, traditions, and customs as forming a binding cement. They object strenuously if by force they were included in a union for which they had no sense of loyalty. They often turn to violence to express their disgust and dismay.

Nationalism remains as a powerful element in all the continents. It is impossible to give attention here to all its manifestations everywhere. It is widespread in the nations of Latin America, where the peoples regard their sense of freedom as disturbed by what they see as an unwarranted interference of the United States in their affairs. When on a 1958 good-will tour in Latin America, Vice President Richard M. Nixon was spat upon by young hotheads in Venezuela, José Figueres, former President of Costa Rica, appeared before a Congressional Committee and issued a statement on why the American President had been received in so insulting a manner. "I must explain that the act of spitting, vulgar though it is, is without substitute in our language for expressing certain emotions." So much for the intensity of Latin American nationalism in facing American nationalism. (*See Reading No. 47.*)

ON THE FUTURE OF NATIONALISM. Although most historians are reluctant to predict the future course of nationalism, there are scholars and journalists who do not hesitate to comment on coming developments. Thus, John Bowle, Professor of Political Theory at the College of Europe in Bruges, Belgium, believes that even though nationalism still persists, it is likely to prove to be only a phase of political development. "We may yet witness the development of the nationalist idea into a world view." (*See Reading No. 48.*)

Journalist Flora Lewis admits that there has been an upsurge of nationalism in recent decades, but she senses that the tide of history is moving against the old instincts. But this renewed wave of nationalism, she believes, comes at a time when independence can be seen as an illusion. In one of her columns for *The New York Times*, she writes that the tide is beginning to rise in a process of change. In her view there may be a new situation in which people may begin to relinquish their previously held and jealously guarded sovereignty. (*See Reading No. 49.*)

By the end of the twentieth century it will be known whether or not nationalism will be rejected as a way of life and cast on the dustbin of history. Certainly at the present time it is very much alive and vital in human affairs. Will the old nationalism of the twentieth century be replaced by a new techno-nationalism? Or will it disappear completely?

Most observant scholars have looked at contemporary nationalism and have found it to be of major importance. Thus, historian John Lukacs wrote these words: "Fifty years later [*after Hitler*] it cannot be denied that nationalism remains the most potent force in the world."[1]

---

[1] John Lukacs, *The Duel: Between Churchill and Hitler* (New York, 1991), p. 223.

PART II

READINGS

READING NO. 1

ERNEST BARKER DEFENDS THE IDEA OF NATIONAL CHARACTER[1]

In the debate over the existence of national character, British scholar Ernest Barker was convinced of its legitimacy. He presented the view that the character of a nation in its formation and its manifestation has its analogies with the character of an individual man. He described national character as a reality, as "a sum of acquire tendencies."

γ   γ   γ

The character of a nation, in its formation and its manifestation, has its analogies with the character of an individual man. Each of us, in his moral growth, starts from a raw stuff of original nature, which is partly a matter of temperament, as determined by bodily structure and its peculiarities, and partly a matter both of inherited instincts common to our general kind and of inherited predispositions common to our immediate stock or family. We shape that raw stuff into a settled form, partly by submission to social discipline, in all its phases, and partly by the repeated exercise of moral choice along lines which gradually become definite and marked. That settled form is character—"the sum of acquired tendencies built upon native bases"; and when it is achieved we have attained both unity of self and permanence of behaviour—we have built an identity which is constant, and expresses itself in what we may call "expectable" action. In much the same way a nation starts from the raw stuff of its material basis; in much the same way it builds upon it a sum of acquired tendencies; in much the same way it settles into the unity and permanence of form which we call by the name of national character. There are indeed differences

---

[1]Ernest Barker, *National Character and the Factors in Its Formation* (New York and London, 1927), pp. 5, 270–271. Courtesy of Harper and Row.

between the nation and the individual. In the first place, we can see the individual as a single physical body, whose character goes, as it were, with his gait and face, and is expressed in obvious and visible actions, which are his, and his alone. We cannot see a nation. It has many members, divided by an infinity of differences; and the unity of its character must be a matter rather of faith than of sight. Yet we can experience if we cannot see; and we somehow know, as Eduard Meyer has said, that "in seizing or despising the possibilities given in each moment a people reveals its individuality, or, in a word, what we call its character." "It is," he adds, "something which we can never explain scientifically in detail, but must accept as a thing which is simply given; and yet it is just this individual and particular element which determines the peculiarity and innermost essence of every historical process."

In the second place, the formation of national character is less a matter of conscious effort and will than the making of individual character. The individual is a single will, acting in the space of a lifetime. The nation is a congeries of wills, acting through centuries. Even an individual, in his measure, moves unconsciously towards the settled form which is his character.

We can experience the character of a nation, as we can experience the personality of an individual; but to describe either, as we can describe a natural object, in terms which will command universal assent, is a task beyond our powers. Individual personality is an opal of many lights, which varies as it is turned to this or that object or person; and national character is no less many-coloured. A nation can hardly see or describe objectively another nation—or indeed, for that matter, itself. The character of the English nation is one thing when it is described by a French writer such as Boutmy; it is another thing when it appears in the pages of a German writer such as Treitschke; it is still another thing when an Englishman seeks to paint the portrait of Englishmen. Prejudice clouds the vision; but prejudice is not the only cloud. There is, or there may be, a bewildering difference between national character as it appears in the individual specimen, and national character as it appears in the conglomerate body of the whole nation. It is less so in France, where an intimate social life and the regulative tradition of the nation have shaped the individual specimen in their own image. It is more so in England, where individual eccentricities of every pattern may play freely around the deep but hidden core of the national being. There *is* a rock on which we stand and from which we are hewn; but we keep it shyly secret in mists of reserve and it is only in some destined hour of national crisis, such as came to us in the midsummer of 1914, that we can see for ourselves, and show to others, the stuff of which we are made.

Yet we can trace, however dimly, some characteristics of our nation. There is a characteristic of energy, partly drawn from the race which predominates in our national blend of races, and partly developed by the influence of the climate in which we live. There is a characteristic of initiative, which a variable climate may have helped to encourage by its shifting demands, but which has been raised to the higher power of a free individuality by a system of common law which has respected the rights of the citizen, a trend of religious thought which has emphasized individual responsibility before God, and an economic doctrine and practice which have remitted to voluntary enterprise the direction of national trade and industry. . . .

READING NO. 2

HAMILTON FYFE ON THE ILLUSION OF NATIONAL CHARACTER[1]

Ernest Barker's defense of the concept of national character was criticized by Hamilton Fyfe, another British scholar. He believed that the concept was merely an illusion and that defense of its existence was doing great harm to the world. He denied that the idea of national character was distinct, homogeneous, and well-defined. It was a dangerous element, in his view, and it could lead to war.

γ   γ   γ

Sir James Frazer has said that every great figure in history is "a harlequin whose particoloured costume differs, according as you look at him from the front or the back, from the right or the left. His friends and his foes behold him from opposite sides, and they naturally see only that particular hue of his coat which happens to be turned towards them."

True as that is of individuals, it is more true of groups, especially true of nations. For the reason that no two individuals are alike. There are no qualities, therefore, which can be said to distinguish a group, such as a club or profession, much less a nation. No one would say: "Doctors are rash or cautious," "Bricklayers are polite or boorish," "Members of the Carlton Club are generous or stingy." Yet, while recognizing that a small group cannot be generalized, almost everybody has until lately taken it for granted that the characteristics of a very large group can be accurately ascertained and set down. This cannot continue. The assumption will not bear analysis. Soon it will be numbered among the popular errors and superstitions that have confused and injured mankind.

[1]Hamilton Fyfe, *The Illusion of National Character* (London, 1940), pp. 3–9. Courtesy of C.A. Watts & Co., Ltd.

A national is not a natural unit, like a herd of buffalo or a pack of wolves. It is largely an accidental unit. The nationality of large numbers has often been changed. The Alsatians have been alternately French and German subjects. But transference did not change their characters, any more than those of the Channel Islanders would be changed if they came under French rule.

"A modern idea and therefore a false idea," Nietzsche said about something (progress, I think). His "therefore" sticks in many throats; it was, like so many of his pronouncements, an over-simplification. Yet, seeing that most ancient ideas appear to us now to be foolish, what reason is there to suppose that our ideas will appear to future ages to have been any truer? One of them, at any rate, which will be laughed at, I am sure, is the illusion of national character.

Or, more probably, it will be looked back on, not with amusement, but with scorn. Scorn such as we feel for belief in the divine rights of kings, or in the enforcement on the world of this or that religion, or in the justice of "trial by ordeal." Scorn for people who could allow their passions to be roused by prickings of national pride and allow wars to be fought as a consequence of those appeals.

By playing upon this folly, rulers have in the past caused immeasurable suffering and ruin. From the time when the Hebrews were told by their fanatical, and therefore slightly demented, leader Moses that they were a "chosen race," appointed to wipe out other races and seize their territory, the idea that nations have characters and missions has frequently tormented and devastated the world.

It is an idea which, so far as I can discover, has never been examined and analysed. It has been uncritically accepted as a fact, though actually it is as much a fiction as the supposed flatness of the earth, the supposed traveling of the sun around the earth, the separate creation of all forms of life, and the differentiation between "the human and the animal kingdoms." All these beliefs, once universally held, are now universally rejected as delusions.

They were allowed to pass for truth because no one challenged them, just as the illusion of national character has been given credence for the reason that it has not been questioned, dissected, exposed. Hardly one of the prominent authors of the late nineteenth and early twentieth centuries doubted that war was a permanent, unavoidable part of the world order. From this they deduced differences between nations, which produced hostility. Certain nations (France and England, Russia and Turkey) they regarded as "natural enemies"; thus they attributed to conflicting temperaments or ideals among the masses what were in fact clashes of material interest among rulers or ruling classes.

This dumb acceptance of evils which we know now to be unnecessary, springing only from Peoples' ignorance and rulers' incapacity or guile, makes the books of even the ablest and most brilliant writers of the Victorian Age seem antiquated. Prof. Karl Pearson, for example, highly regarded as teacher and philosopher, laid it down that "there is a struggle of race against race, and nation against nation," and that "a national spirit was wholly good" if it took the form of "a strong feeling of the importance of organizing the nation as a whole, of making its social and economic conditions such that it is able to do its work in the world and meet its fellows without hesitation in the field" (that is, the battlefield) "or the market."[2]

Nations, it seemed to Karl Pearson, must be "organized wholes in continual struggle with other nations, whether by force of arms or by force of trade and other economic processes"; and this was not a wholly bad thing, since it was the "source of human progress throughout the world's history."

Another Pearson (C. H.) about the same period went from England to Australia, became Minister of Education in the State of Victoria, and after his return wrote a book called *National Life and Character*, which was earnestly discussed, as it deserved to be. He foresaw the advance of Socialism, but he did not anticipate any federation of Socialist States which would eliminate the risk of war between them. He predicted that "every State will have to be constantly on its guard against dismemberment or subjugation." That prediction at this moment has come true.

[2]*National Life from the Standpoint of Science*, 1901.

Where his book seems old-fashioned when we read it to-day is in the writer's failure to throw his glance forward to a time when there would not any longer be this perpetual armed watchfulness, burdensome in its cost and disastrous in drawing energy away from wholesome activities.

Recent writers have been little more discerning. Prof. Ernest Barker, who published in 1927 a book on *National Character and the Factors in its Formation*, did not begin by asking whether there was such a thing as national character; he took it for granted and expected his readers to do the same.

His definition was—

National character is the sum of acquired tendencies, built up by leaders in every sphere of activity, with the consent and co-operation, active in some, but more or less passive in others, of the general community.

Prof. Barker does not include inherited tendencies, yet these, as factors of national character, are proclaimed more insistently than elements acquired or implanted by schooling and patriotic propaganda. By ignoring them Prof. Barker showed that he had a clearer understanding of his subject than he set down in his book. But only by inference could the reader gather this. . . .

Men and women who easily change their minds, their sympathies, are said to be weather cocks, to lack character. Apply the same reasoning to nations and it will be seen that, since no nation can show a consistent line of action, none have national characters.

READING NO. 3

HANS J. MORGENTHAU ON NATIONALISM IN THE ATOMIC AGE[1]

The late Hans J. Morgenthau, distinguished political scientist, was concerned with the nature of nationalism and wrote much about it. He was unaware about the danger of predicting its future. Venturing into the field of prophecy, he expressed the feeling that nationalism has had its day and is no longer a viable institution in the contemporary world.

γ   γ   γ

Nationalism has had its day. It was the political principle appropriate to the post-feudal and pre-atomic age. For the technology of the steam engine, it was indeed in good measure a force for progress. In the atomic age, it must make way for a political principle of larger dimensions, in tune with the world-wide configurations of interest and power of the age.

[1]From Hans J. Morgenthau, *The Dilemma of Politics* (Chicago, 1958), p. 172. Courtesy of University of Chicago Press.

READING NO. 4

KARL W. DEUTSCH ON BEYOND THE FENCES OF NATION-STATES[1]

Another political scientist, Karl W. Deutsch, sees the whole thrust of technological development in the contemporary world as beyond wars and the economic fences of nation-states.

γ   γ   γ

The whole thrust of the technological development of our time pushes beyond wars and beyond the economic fences of nation-states. It seems to push toward a pluralistic world of limited international law, limited, but growing, international cooperation, and regional pluralistic security communities. In a few favored regions these may even give place to regional federations, but this will be a slow development. The future also seems to promise considerably increased voluntary redistribution of income through economic cooperation and the equivalent of an international income tax.

These developments may get us through the valley of the shadow of death. They may preserve us, individuals and nations, for the next three or four decades, in which nuclear war is all too possible. Peace *can* be had in our time. It has behind it the pressure of technology, the necessity of survival, and the longing of millions of human beings everywhere in the world. We can have this peace in the next two generations—if we believe in the future, and if we are willing to work for it.

[1]Karl W. Deutsch, *Nationalism and Its Alternatives*, (New York, 1989), p. 190. By permission of Alfred A. Knopf, Inc.

READING NO. 5

E. J. HOBSBAWM SEES NATIONS AS A NUISANCE[1]

In his latest book, Nations and Nationalism Since 1780, *British Marxist historian E. J. Hobsbawm sees nations as a nuisance and claims that "nationalism is no longer a major vector of historical development." Stanley Hoffmann, chairman of the Center for European Studies at Harvard University, reviewed Hobsbawm's book for* The New York Times *and found the author's verdict on nationalism as wrong and unacceptable.*

γ   γ   γ

. . . This is one of the reasons why he proclaims that nationalism "is no longer a major vector of historical development"—a conclusion that owes at least as much to Mr. Hobsbawm's own hostility to it as to the march of events. Since as a rational social scientist he has a tendency to believe that "objective" criteria of nationality such as language or ethnicity are "fuzzy, shifting and ambiguous," and that subjective definitions (in terms of common will or consciousness of belonging) are "tautological," Mr. Hobsbawm finds national identification, when it is intense, something of an obnoxious nuisance. He is right in arguing that it does not exclude other identifications. But by adopting a definition of nationalism as "a principle which holds that the political and the national unit should be congruent," he confuses three very different things: national consciousness (or patriotism), the principle of nationality (to each nation its state) and the ideology of nationalism (my nation, right or wrong). . . .

[1]E. J. Hobsbawm's *Nations and Internationalism Since 1780* (New York, 1990), reviewed by Stanley Hoffmann, in *The New York Times Book Review* (October 7, 1990), pp. 24–25. Copyright © by The New York Times Company. Reprinted by permission.

At the beginning of his second chapter, Mr. Hobsbawm asks: "Why and how could a concept so remote from the real experience of most human beings as 'national patriotism' become such a powerful political force so quickly?" Earlier he had stated that "no serious historian of nations and nationalism can be a committed political nationalist." If commitments necessarily lead to bias in scholarship, he is right. But the absence of, indeed the dislike of, a commitment, can lead even the most learned of writers to a kind of obtuseness, from lack of empathy (different, incidentally, from sympathy or endorsement). Mr. Hobsbawm on nationalism is a bit like a deaf man writing about music.

READING NO. 6

HANS KOHN ON THE IMPACT OF NATIONALISM[1]

Hans Kohn, along with Carlton J. H. Hayes, an American pioneer scholar of nationalism, spent his entire career on its study. In many books and articles he stressed its extraordinarily powerful role in modern history and at the same time called attention to its divisive force in world affairs. He saw nationalism as the determining political and cultural force among all the races and civilizations on earth.

γ   γ   γ

Nationalism has been one of the determining forces in modern history. It originated in eighteenth century Western Europe; during the nineteenth century it spread all over Europe; in the twentieth century it has become a world-wide movement, and its importance in Asia and Africa is growing with every year. But nationalism is not the same in all countries and at all times. It is a historical phenomenon and thus determined by the political ideas and the social structure of the various lands where it takes root.

An understanding of nationalism and its implications for modern history and for our time appears as fundamental today as an understanding of religion would have been for thirteenth century Christendom. Like religion, nationalism can present many and most diverse forms. Only a study of the historical growth of nationalism and a comparative study of its different forms can make us understand the impact of nationalism today, the promise and the peril which it has carried and continues to carry for the liberty of man and the preservation of peace. . . .

[1]Hans Kohn, *Nationalism: Its Meaning and History* (Princeton, N.J., 1955), pp. 4, 88, 89. Courtesy of D. van Nostrand Co., Inc.

The twentieth century is the first period in history, in which the whole of mankind has accepted one and the same political attitude, that of nationalism. Its rise everywhere implied an activization of the people and the demand for a new ordering of society. But everywhere nationalism differs in character according to the specific historic conditions and the peculiar social structure of each country. World-wide nationalism has, however, not simplified or facilitated the task of creating a cohesive and cooperative human society. Outside Turkey none of the Middle Eastern and Asian nations had reached by 1955 a degree of political and economic stability which would presage the secure growth of civil liberties and social reform. National and imperial ambitions among Asian peoples threaten to clash as they have among European nations. China has in no way been willing to grant national independence to Tibet or to the Mohammedan peoples in Sinkiang; on the contrary, it is trying to reassert its former imperial influence in Korea and Annam. Chinese settlers throughout Southeast Asia and Indian settlers in Eastern Africa, both enjoying the protection of their lands of origin, may create difficulties recalling imperial conflicts of the recent past. With the promotion under British leadership of new African nations in Nigeria and the Gold Coast to independence and with the cultural and social emancipation of the Indian element in many Latin American countries—a process in which Mexico through the new Constitution of January 31, 1917 and the "Aztec renaissance" has led the way—nationalism has become the determining political and cultural force among all the races and civilizations on earth.

Though thus establishing a common world-wide element, nationalism is a deeply divisive force, if it is not tempered by the liberal spirit of tolerance and compromise or the humanitarian universalism of a non-political religion. Its stress upon national sovereignty and cultural distinctiveness hardly helps to promote cooperation among peoples at the very time when for technological and economic reasons they grow more and more interdependent.

READING NO. 7

BOYD C. SHAFER ON THE NEVER-ENDING CIRCLE OF NATIONALISM[1]

Although the distinguished American scholar of nationalism, Boyd C. Shafer, expressed the hope for a world-state, a truly international order above the nations, his analysis of nationalism in its present form saw a never-ending circle. In his view nationalism in the contemporary world has become self-perpetuating, each nationalism living and growing in imitation and fear of other nationalisms.

γ   γ   γ

Almost every activity and idea seemed to conspire to promote nationalism. Ideas re-enforced national institutions. These institutions fostered national ideas. How could men enlarge their freedoms, obtain protection against the vicissitudes of everyday life or foreign enemies? Through unity of thought and action within their own nations. What once king, noble, and priest provided for them in the way of protection, the independent national state could do and do more completely and efficiently. Outside the state, though increasingly brought within it, economic forces and cultural influences worked toward the same national ends. Railroads stitched the Italian boot, made possible the economic cohesiveness upon which Mazzini, Garibaldi, and Cavour could politically unify Italy. In the United States, Henry Clay's "American system," and similar schemes brought the sections together. Everywhere tariffs protected national eco-

[1]Boyd C. Shafer, *Nationalism: Interpreters and Interpretation* (Washington, D.C., 1959), pp. 10–12. (Publication No. 20: Service Center for Teachers of History, American Historical Association.) This pamphlet was a revised version of an article, "Nationalism—Some Myths and Realities," published in *The Journal of International Affairs*, Vol. XII, No. 2, 1958. By permission of Boyd C. Shafer.

nomic interests. Banking systems became national and, later, great industries became national industries with plants and sales covering the nation. All these chiefly protected and aided business. But workers and farmers became involved, as well, as they demanded, and over the years usually obtained, protection against foreign labor or crops, as they received social insurance or crop loans, and as they were guaranteed minimum wages or parity prices.

Men do not necessarily love the hand that feeds them or worship their benefactors. Indeed some men have fought against the pervading patriotism and resisted the power of the Leviathan national states. The fact remains that over the world men have become increasingly national-minded. When the Negro in the United States wanted equality, he asks action by the national government because he thinks that he cannot get this equality through any other agency. When the Hungarians want rights today, they believe that they must throw off Russian domination and obtain Hungarian independence. They know no other way. For the achievement of needs and desires, for order and safety, the nation seems to be the modern means.

Everything the citizen hears and sees seems to re-enforce this observation. The radio is national, television is national. The schools teach national citizenship. The historians chiefly teach and write national histories. Literature and cooking and sports are judged on national criteria. Even science and music, written in international notation and symbol, becomes Russian, German, French, or American rather than just science and music. To make certain that national values rather than others prevail, patriotic societies in every country demand with some success that foreign influences be rooted out, that only good national or "one hundred per cent" ideas be encouraged. A man does not necessarily love his benefactor, but in this case he has not much opportunity to do otherwise.

The nation-state has hence often become an end in itself, the one end, indeed, socially approved for the supreme sacrifice. It can and often does in our contemporary world, control everything a man does or thinks, especially in times of national emergencies. The most extreme nationalisms of our time, those of Hitler and Mussolini, grew out of war, lived on war or probability of war, and themselves made war. Here we see nationalism self-perpetuating, each nationalism living and growing in imitation and in fear of other nationalisms. To beat Naziism and fascism, as Goebbels and the Nazis predicted, other nations unfortunately had to become somewhat like them. "The true nationalist," the French newspaper *L'Action Fran-çaise* once declared, "places the fatherland above everything." Not all men in the twentieth century were "true nationalists" in this ultimate sense, but the pressures which conditioned them were relentlessly pushing them in that direction.

Is there no way out of this neverending circle, whether it is vicious or not? I am a historian. I cannot predict. If we are to have, at any future time, a truly international order above the nations, or if we are to have a world state, the international or world government will have to grow as national governments did, and if it is to have substance and viability, if indeed it is to exist, it will have to touch the vital interests of each world citizen. It, too, will have to grow, as nationalism did, out of the concrete fears and hopes, desires and actions of people who are passionately interested in its maintenance for their own freedom and safety. It will, too, have to afford the promise of a better life and, at the same time, protect man in the ways national governments have. But whether this can or will happen, whether or not we have time in this age of national hydrogen bombs, I do not know.

The reality of nationalism is the feeling of people, a feeling based upon each people's historical myths and realities. The reality of the nation lies in the hope and freedom, the protection and security it affords. If nationalism is to be succeeded by some new loyalty, to a world religion or a world state, some other realities, some new myths will have to provide as much and touch the citizens of the present nations as deeply.

READING NO. 8

COUDENHOVE-KALERGI: CHAMPION OF A UNITED EUROPE[1]

The moving spirit behind Pan-Europa was the Austrian Richard N. Coudenhove-Kalergi. Moved by the thought that nationalism was a terrifying force and must be challenged for the benefit of humanity, he devoted his life to the task of combatting it and working for a united Europe. The following reading shows how he struggled to implement his belief.

γ   γ   γ

The human animal is a persistent creature. Again and again a loner appears who is so convinced of the sacred truth of his cause that he transforms advocacy into a crusade. Such a man was the Austrian Count Richard N. Coudenhove-Kalergi, who during the Long Armistice between the two World Wars, projected his federalist Pan-Europa. Small in stature but a giant in resolution, he received little popular support for his movement, but that made no difference to a fiery zealot.

Of mixed parentage, Coudenhove-Kalergi was born in Tokyo on November 16, 1894, the son of the *chargé-d'affaires* in the Austro-Hungarian embassy and Mitsui Aoyama, an upper-class Japanese girl fifteen years younger than her husband. The boy grew up in Bohemia in a household that included nine nationalities. Early in life he became convinced that nationalism was a dangerous historical phenomenon, and that cooperation should be the goal of all civilized human beings. In his view, nationalism was "a terrifying force," and it might continue to exist for centuries to come.

While studying in Vienna for his doctorate, Coudenhove-Kalergi was appalled by the Pan-Germanism advocated by his

[1]From Louis L. Snyder, *Macro-Nationalisms: A History of the Pan-Movements* (Westport, Ct., 1984), pp. 74–76. Courtesy of Greenwood Press, Westport, Ct.

fellow students, and especially by the rampant anti-Semitism in Viennese circles. Exempt from military service in World War I because of a lung condition, he became a passionate Wilsonian after the entry of the United States into the war. After the war he became an ardent advocate of the League of Nations, and regarded himself as a citizen of the world. He decided to work "not for one country but for the brotherhood of man." He was saddened by the inability of the League to rise above "the law of the jungle" in relations between twenty-six nations of Europe. What was needed desperately, in his view, was a federated Europe on the model of the United States and Switzerland. To implement that goal became his lifelong pursuit.

Coudenhove-Kalergi was convinced that the League of Nations could not possibly work without U.S. participation. He urged the reorganization of the League into six autonomous regional units—the British Commonwealth, the Soviet Union, Pan-Europa, Pan-America, China, and Japan. There could be no united world, he warned, with a disunited Europe. League officials were not impressed. They saw the suggestion as contrary to the spirit of a world organization.

Undiscouraged, Coudenhove-Kalergi went ahead with his one-man crusade. In 1922, he presented the first draft of his program for Pan-Europa in the *Neue Freie Press* (Vienna) and the *Vossische Zeitung* (Berlin). He then began to search for the support of important sponsors. Walther Rathenau, Thomas Masaryk, and Joseph Caillaux, all distinguished statesmen, gave him encouragement, but did not or could not head his movement. He appealed to Mussolini to help promote a European federation, but was met by uncharacteristic silence. He decided to go on alone.

Coudenhove-Kalergi began publishing a long series of books on the Pan-Europa idea. He traveled throughout Europe delivering lectures for his cause. He enlisted the support of Winston Churchill, Aristide Briand, José Ortega y Gasset, and others. Coming to the United States in 1925, he reorganized the American Cooperative Committee for the Pan-European Union under the chairmanship of the educator Dr. Stephen Pierce Duggan, head of the Institute of International Education.

Convinced that he was making headway, Coudenhove-Kalergi in October 1926 called the Pan-European Congress in

Vienna, the first of a series of such meetings. Twenty-four hundred supporters from many European nations attended the gathering, and unanimously elected Coudenhove-Kalergi as President of the Pan-European Union.

The Second Pan-European Congress was convened in Berlin in May 1930. This time there was considerably less enthusiasm. The British, still obsessed with the old traditional balance of power, blocked Briand's efforts for union. The Germans, with Stresemann dead, seemed to have lost sympathy for the European idea.

The third Pan-European Congress, held at Basel in 1932, was overshadowed by the menacing rise of Nazism. Coudenhove-Kalergi denounced Hitler and National Socialism, for he deplored the revival of Pan-Germanism with a Nazi tinge. As soon as he came to power in 1933, Hitler struck back by banning the German Pan-European Union.

The Fourth Pan-European Congress convened in Vienna in May 1935, the Fifth Congress in November 1937. Coudenhove-Kalergi called for the introduction of Pan-European schools, as well as for the elimination of duties on agricultural goods. This was the first projection of the Common Market idea. . . .

In March 1939, after ordering an invasion of Czechoslovakia in flat defiance of his Munich pledge, Hitler proclaimed annexation of the country. Coudenhove-Kalergi opted for French citizenship. He called for an international meeting for European union, while at the same time working for Pan-Europeanism among delegates of the French Chamber of Deputies. In April 1940 he called on the French Pan-European Committee to achieve Franco-British unity. After the fall of France, he left for the United States.

As research associate in history at New York University, Coudenhove-Kalergi headed a Seminar for Postwar European Federation. In March 1943, shortly after Churchill had made a speech favoring a United States of Europe, Coudenhove-Kalergi called the Sixth Pan-European Congress. The next year he drew up a constitution for a United States of Europe, and submitted it to all the heads and foreign ministers of nations represented in the United Nations. He included provisions for a central European bank; unification of the European transportation system; European free trade; a Continental customs union; a federal army; a "House of States" with one delegate for each small nation and two for each large one; a House of Representatives with one to ten delegates per state; an Executive Council elected by both houses and consisting of one delegate per state; a President elected for a one-year term; and Supreme Court judges appointed by the Executive Council.

In 1947, at a meeting held at Gstaad, Switzerland, the European Parliamentary Union was founded with Coudenhove-Kalergi as Secretary-General. The passionate crusader seemed to be making progress.

There was, however, an underlying weakness. Coudenhove-Kalergi's idea of Pan-Europa attracted the attention and support of like-minded intellectuals, but, unfortunately, it lacked a mass base. This did not deter the energetic Austrian, nor was he discouraged when European statesmen returned to the dangerous traditions of prewar diplomacy. But the impulse for Pan-Europa began to pass to other hands.

Eventually, Coudenhove-Kalergi's draft constitution for a United States of Europe was to be realized in the formation of the European Parliament. However, this institution was to become an ineffective extension of economic union. Neither Coudenhove-Kalergi nor the European Parliament succeeded in winning mass support for Pan-Europa.

READING NO. 9

ROBERT SCHUMAN ON THE EUROPEAN COAL AND STEEL COMMUNITY[1]

On May 9, 1950, French statesman Robert Schuman predicted that the pooling of European coal and steel production would establish the basis for a European confederation indispensable for the safeguarding of peace.

γ   γ   γ

Europe will not be built at once or through a single comprehensive plan. It will be built through concrete achievements, which will first create a *de facto* solidarity. The comity of European nations requires that the rivalry of France and Germany should be eliminated. . . . The pooling of the production of coal and steel will immediately establish a common basis for economic development.

Thus will be realized, simply and rapidly, the fusion of interests which will be indispensable for establishing an economic community between countries long opposed by bloody conflict. This will establish the basis for a European confederation indispensable for the safeguarding of peace.

[1]Walter Farr, *"Daily Telegraph" Guide to the Common Market* (London, 1972), p. 24. Courtesy of the *Daily Telegraph*.

READING NO. 10

FOUNDING OF THE EUROPEAN ECONOMIC UNION[1]

The European Economic Community (E.E.C.) was founded by the Treaty of Rome on March 25, 1957. The text contained not only the basis for the Common Market, but outlined additional policies intended to lead to full economic union of European nations. The goals were stated in the preamble.

γ   γ   γ

HIS MAJESTY THE KING OF THE BELGIANS, THE PRESIDENT OF THE FEDERAL REPUBLIC OF WEST GERMANY, THE PRESIDENT OF THE FRENCH REPUBLIC, THE PRESIDENT OF THE ITALIAN REPUBLIC, HER ROYAL HIGHNESS THE GRAND DUCHESS OF LUXEMBOURG, HER MAJESTY THE QUEEN OF THE BELGIANS.

DETERMINED to establish the foundations of an ever closer union among European peoples,

RESOLVED to ensure by common action the economic and social progress of their countries by eliminating the barriers which divide Europe,

AFFIRMING as the essential objective of their efforts the constant improvement of the living and working conditions of their peoples,

RECOGNISING that the removal of existing obstacles calls for constant action in order to guarantee steady expansion, balanced trade and fair competition,

ANXIOUS to strengthen the unity of their economies and to ensure their harmonious development by reducing the differ-

---

[1] Walter Farr, *"Daily Telegraph" Guide to the Common Market* (London, 1972), p. 33. Courtesy of the *Daily Telegraph*.

ences existing between the various regions and the backwardness of the less favored regions,

DESIRING to contribute, by means of a common commercial policy, to the progressive abolition of restrictions on international trade,

INTENDING to confirm the solidarity which binds Europe and overseas countries and desiring to ensure the development of their prosperity, in accordance with the principles of the Charter of the United Nations,

RESOLVED to strengthen the cause of peace and liberty by thus pooling resources and calling upon the other peoples of Europe who share their ideal to join in their efforts,

HAVE DECIDED to create a European Economic Community.

READING NO. 11

SHAKESPEARE AND THE POWERFUL APPEAL OF ENGLISH PATRIOTISM[1]

The tremendous appeal of love for the land was shown as early as 1595 by Shakespeare in The Tragedy of King Richard the Second. *As he lay dying, John of Gaunt gave this stirring address to King Richard in which he uttered the famous line: "This blessed plot, this earth, this realm, this England." This patriotic theme became the backbone of English nationalism and helps explain its continued existence.*

γ   γ   γ

This royal throne of kings, this scepter'd isle,
This earth of majesty, this seat of Mars,
This other Eden, demi-paradise,
This fortress built by Nature for herself
Against infection and the hand of war,
This happy breed of men,this little world,
This precious stone set in the silver sea,
Which serves it in the office of a wall,
Or as a moat defensive to a house,
Against the envy of less happier lands,
This blessed plot, this earth, this realm, this England,
This nurse, this teeming womb of royal kings,
Fear'd by their breed and famous by their birth,
Renowned for their deeds as far from home,—
For Christian service and true chivalry,—
As is the sepulchre in stubborn Jewry
Of the world's ransom, blessed Mary's Son:
This land of such dear souls, this dear, dear land,
Dear for her reputation, through the world. . . .

[1]*The Histories and Poems of Shakespeare* (London, 1912), pp. 107–108.

READING NO. 12

CHARLES DE GAULLE AND
FRENCH NATIONALISM[1]

*For Charles de Gaulle, French resistance leader in World War
II, France was not merely a* patrie, *it was a mystique. He
identified the nation with himself: "And today I was at the head
of a ruined, decimated, lacerated nation, surrounded by ill-will.
Hearing my voice, France has been able to unite and march to
her liberation."*

γ   γ   γ

Our country, with her tinted sky, her varied contours, her
fertile soil, her fields full of fine corn and vines and livestock,
our industry, our gifts of initiative, adaptation, and self-respect,
make us, above all others, a race created for brilliant deeds
(1934).

The emotional side of me tends to imagine France, like the
princess in the stories or Madonnas in the frescoes, as dedicated
to an exalted and exceptional destiny. But the positive side of my
mind also assures me that France is not really herself unless in
the front rank; that only vast enterprises are capable of counter-
balancing the divisive ferments which are inherent in her people. In short, in my mind, France cannot be France without
greatness (1955).

[1]Quoted in *Time*, February 8, 1963, p. 23. Copyright 1963, The Time, Inc.
Magazine Company. Reprinted by permission.

READING NO. 13

MARGARET THATCHER VERSUS THE EUROCRATS[1]

Journalist George F. Will commented on former Prime Minister Margaret Thatcher's "matriarchal machismo" in her stand against European federalism. Her view: when sovereignty and Parliament's rights shrink what becomes of democracy?

γ   γ   γ

In 1988 in Bruges, near Brussels, the bureaucratic headquarters of Brave New Europe, [Margaret Thatcher] denounced efforts to "suppress nationhood and consolidate power at the center of a European conglomerate": "We have not successfully rolled back the frontiers of the state in Britain, only to see them reimposed at a European level, with a European superstate exercising a new dominance from Brussels." She was responding to Jacques Delors, who enjoys "chief of state" (what state?) status but who is only the appointed head of the European Community's unelected executive commission. Delors says that soon 80 percent of Europe's economic and perhaps social legislation "will be of Community origin. . . ."

Thatcher's words at Bruges were very British. Here is Harold Macmillan in Strasbourg in 1950: "Fearing the weakness of democracy, men have often sought safety in technocrats. But . . . [the British] have not overthrown the divine right of kings to fall down before the divine right of experts." Must the ascending march that began 775 years ago on Runnymede Meadow end with the ascendancy of Brussels' Eurocrats? Thatcher's "no!" will reverberate.

[1]From *Newsweek*, December 3, 1990, p. 74, © 1990. Newsweek, Inc. All rights reserved. Reprinted by permission.

READING NO. 14

REPORTS ON THE GRIM SITUATION IN THE SOVIET UNION[1]

In 1990, comments on the situation in the Soviet Union were invariably pessimistic. The first report below from Time *shows how economic backwardness has fueled resentment against central authority. The second, from* Newsweek, *reveals how nationalism threatens civil unrest and how Soviet citizens face a future bleak and uncertain.*

γ   γ   γ

I Unrest in the Multinational Empire. From Estonia on the Baltic Sea to Tadzhikistan in the Pamir mountains of Central Asia, the Soviet Union is coming apart at the seams. The U.S.S.R. as such might soon cease to exist. In its place may be a smaller, though still vast, country, perhaps called simply Russia, while Estonia and Tadzhikistan could be two of a dozen or more Soviet republics that become independent countries. If that happens, the world will have lost not only its first communist state but also its last great multinational empire. . . .

Much of the survival of the Soviet Union in its present form is threatened by unrest among its non-Russian minorities. . . .

Like the Turkish empire, the Soviet Union suffers from economic backwardness, which has fueled resentment of central authority and, in the past several years, secessionism. Seeking the fruits of technology and commerce, restive nationalities turn away from Moscow and toward the outside world.

[1](1) *Time*, October 29, 1990, p. 93. Copyright 1990, The Time Inc. Magazine Company. Reprinted by permission. (2) *Newsweek*, December 11, 1990, p. 34, and copyright © Newsweek, Inc. All rights reserved. Reprinted by permission.

II Emigration Psychosis. As food shortages spread through-out the Soviet Union and nationalism threatens civil unrest, Soviet citizens face a future both bleak and uncertain. And increasingly, nearby Europeans fear the result. From Helsinki to Budapest, governments are bracing for a demographic deluge. Finnish officials warn that as many as 2 million Soviets might try to cross their 775-mile border this winter. Poland and Czechoslovakia are turning former Soviet Army barracks into emergency refugee camps. German officials speak uneasily of deploying the Army to keep unwanted foreigners out. Germany absorbed a million immigrants from the Soviet Union and Eastern Europe this year; that figure could swell fivefold, officials say, if conditions in the East deteriorate drastically.

The Germans call it *Völkerwanderung* (migration of peoples). But for all the panicky talk, it's hard to gauge the true dimen-sions of the threat. "This is a psychological crisis, a fad," scoffs one European Community official, dismissing fears of a mass migration as "wildly exaggerated." Powerful forces militate against a flood. Even as German relief planes unloaded in Leningrad and Moscow last week, it was clear the Soviet Union faces not an outright famine, but endemic shortages caused by distribution bottlenecks. And though the Soviet Parliament is expected to pass new laws allowing its citizens to travel freely, the legislation will not take effect for at least six months.

Even then the fine print will be discouraging; Soviets seeking to leave, for instance, will have to forfeit most of their savings and belongings. Under current law, an estimated 500,000 So-viets will have emigrated by the year-end, and most of these consider themselves oppressed minorities, such as Jews and ethnic Germans.

READING NO. 15

THE COURSE OF ESTONIAN NATIONALISM[1]

How the Estonians reacted to Soviet rule imposed by Stalin is described in this article by Marika Kirch and Aksel Kirch, senior research fellows of the National Process in Estonia research program. Estonians see this period as an era of ethnocide. The attitude was similar in the entire Baltic region.

γ   γ   γ

Analysing Estonian society today, we can see that certain restrictions operated on the social processes during the course of the last fifty years. The turning point for Estonian national development came in 1940 when the Estonian Republic was incorporated into the Soviet Union. From that time on one must interpret Estonian social development by taking into consideration specific features of the changing situation in Soviet society in general.

The Soviet period in Estonian history (from the point of national policy) may be analysed as consisting of two significant periods that have profound influence on today's situation: first, the direct repressions of the Stalinist period (1940–1956). (Today, this period is characterized by Estonians as the period of genocide and ethnocide.) Secondly, there was the period of concealed repressions (from the beginning of 1970 to 1985). Today this period is interpreted as the period of stagnation and unification. To repeat, these two periods are of utmost significance to contemporary development of Estonian society. . . .

The national problem in Estonia is mainly the result of the

[1]M. Kirch and A. Kirch, "The National Process in Estonia Today," *Nationalities Papers*, Vol. XVI, No. 2 (Fall, 1988), pp. 171–172, 175–176. The editors are from the Academy of Sciences, Estonia. By permission of the *Nationalities Papers*.

nationality policy of the last forty-nine years. Till 1985 the Estonian government and the Communist Party leaders implemented the principles of official ideology whose aim was the formation of a unified Soviet people, with no differences and specific features between the various nations. . . .

In the economical sphere Estonians harbor much more pessimistic attitudes regarding national processes in Estonia today. At the same time, while Estonians hold generally pessimistic attitudes towards future relations, the normally optimistic attitudes of Russians and other nations that dominated in 1986 have decreased markedly.

At this point, it is necessary to explain the essence of the phenomenon "internationalism," for, during the last decades, this notion has been made use of extraordinarily often. We think that internationalism is expressed in the attitude towards all nations (ethnic units) as equi-important, in which the characteristics uniting people are of higher value than those separating them. . . .

In fact, under the slogan of "internationalism," an intensive process of assimilation was and still is being carried out. At the same time the so-called great-power ideology which proceeds from the wrong interpretation of internationalism is of such a great influence, that not only small nations (for example Karelians, Mordvidians, Chuvash) but also big ones (Ukrainians, Byelorussians) are being assimilated. During recent years the new political assimilation of small nations, carried out under the slogan of protecting the unitary state, has been added to the traditional assimilation model. In fact it is the unification of culture and language.

We conclude that the national process must be analysed on two levels: First, the level of national policy—the relations between the nations as ethnic-cultural systems, in which the main issue is the protection of national interests: secondly, the level of interethnic relations as being individuals. The essential matter of this latter level is mutual understanding and respect between different nations, overcoming mutual communication barriers and attitudes. In essence, it is a psychological problem.

The present radical reorganization of Soviet society today offers an opportunity for the resolution of problems stemming from past nationality policy. It is absolutely necessary to proceed from specific historic and political contexts when designing a more humanistic nationality policy which takes into account the whole complexity of the national development process, as is the case in Estonia today.

READING NO. 16

CONSTRUCTION OF A MULTI-NATIONAL SOVIET FEDERALISM[1]

How the Soviets constructed their administrative "socialist federalism" was the subject of this study in 1986 by Alexander Shtromas. The author shows how this multi-national policy failed to reconcile the nations thus ruled. By 1990 it became obvious that this attempt to rule a heterogeneous community failed when its component parts thrust their sense of nationalism against the centralized nationalism of the Kremlin.

γ   γ   γ

The Soviet approach to multinationalism is based on the USSR's administrative-political division into national-territorial units which, regardless of size and population, are formally accorded equal status and rights. The Soviet Union is divided into fifteen "equal" union republics, each bearing the name of a different nation. Furthermore, a few multi-national union republics contain—alongside territorial administrative-political units, such as territory (*kray*), province (*oblast'*), city (*gorod*), and district (*rayon*)—specific national-territorial units: autonomous republic, autonomous province, and autonomous region (*okrug*). Each unit accommodates nations and nationalities having "sub-union-republican status." The former two are structured as separate administrative-political units directly subordinated to the union-republic's authority, whereas the latter functions within a certain administrative territory or province and is subordinated to the sub-republican local authority. The arrangement whereby nationally definable territorial areas en-

---

[1]Alexander Shtromas, "The Building of a Multi-National 'Socialist Federalism': Success and Failures," in *Canadian Review of Studies in Nationalism*, Vol. XIII, No. 1 (Spring, 1986), pp. 79–81, 95–96. By permission of the *Canadian Review of Studies in Nationalism*.

joy priority in devising the country's administrative-political structure forms the essence of "socialist federalism." . . .

The Russian Republic contains sixteen autonomous republics, five autonomous provinces, and all of the country's ten autonomous regions. In view of this vast variety of nations and the thirty-one territorial units assigned to them, Russia is a "Federal Soviet Socialist Republic" in its own right within the socialist federal structure of the USSR. However, certain other union-republics not accorded such special status also contain separate national territorial units. The Georgian SSR has two autonomous republics and one autonomous province, the Azerbaijanian SSR has one autonomous republics and one autonomous province, the Uzbek SSR has one autonomous republic, and the Tadjik SSR has one autonomous province. Altogether, the USSR's union republics contain thirty-eight national-territorial units which, in addition to the fifteen union republics, are directly represented in the Soviet of Nationalities, one of the two "equal-rights" Houses of the USSR's Supreme Soviet—the country's official Parliament.

Each of the USSR's fifty-three national-territorial units provides some room for the development and self-assertion of ethnic entities whose name, or names, these units bear. Local national languages are in official usage, in addition to Russian, the state language of the Soviet Union. In national schools, where Russian is the second language, certain elements of the national history and cultural tradition are taught, and in each such unit, officially sanctioned cultural institutions dispense selective aspects of the national heritage. In most instances, the media usage of national languages is dominant, and native literatures of the "socialist realism" variety are generously sponsored by the authorities.

The founding fathers of the Soviet system conceived "socialist federalism" as a political structure capable of replacing the traditional imperial-colonial model of a multinational state which hitherto, with few exceptions (*i.e.*, Switzerland), was the only model history had known. Its framers believed it would help abolish inter-national suspicions and antagonisms and draw nations ever closer until they gradually merged into one supranational Soviet socialist people eventually able to embrace all of mankind. The Soviet "socialist-federalist" experiment con-

tinues, but after more than six decades, it has failed to fulfill the
expectations of its creators. It would be futile to explain this
failure by seeking inadequacies or shortcomings within the
formal structure of Soviet "socialist federalism." In fact, this
conception was sufficiently imaginative and innovative to lend
some hope towards satisfactorily accommodating different nations within a single political unit, and thus providing a significant departure from the prevalent imperial-colonial tradition" . . .

Soviet national policy aimed at "drawing together" the Soviet
nations has merely united them in a common sense of resentment and rejection of the Soviet multinational state. The deep
animosity between the Russians and non-Russians notwith-
standing, nationalist dissenters of whatever party realize their
fundamental unity of purpose, and as an anonymous Soviet
dissident aptly expresses it: "The preposterous Marxist slogan
proletarians of all countries, unite, was definitively and irrever-
sibly replaced in the USSR by the only realistic and operational
one: nationalists of all nations, unite" . . .

If authority should collapse for reasons quite remote from the
purely national, all nations within the USSR and those under its
control would, for the first time, acquire an opportunity to assert
themselves as genuinely autonomous entities, thus bringing to a
close the system of "socialist federalism." Valeriya Novod-
vorskaya, a prominent dissident Russian poet, has succinctly
phrased this idea:

> What can one see there, in that remote blueness,
> Behind the line of dawn?
> Most probably Russia,
> Certainly not the country of the Soviets.

Not only restored national Russia resides "behind the line of
dawn," but also the genuine nation-states of Georgia, Uzbeki-
stan, Lithuania, and many others.

Soviet national policy, in general, and the federal arrangement of the Soviet state, in particular, have produced a highly
effective, perhaps even an ideal, instrument of firm, centralized
rule over a multinational country. It has failed, however, to
reconcile the nations thus ruled, so that the gradual development
of a homogeneous community of Soviet people might be

achieved. The nations residing under conditions imposed by the Soviet regime have proven unmergeable (or, to paraphrase Soviet official terminology, "*unsliyable*"), and, currently, nothing short of brute force would deprive them of firmly entrenched separate national identities. The persistent and sharpening multinationalism of the USSR is a time-bomb ticking beneath the surface of the illusory Soviet monolith. A force sufficiently powerful to defuse it is difficult to visualize.

READING NO. 17

SOVIET SOCIETY AS A JUMBLE OF LANGUAGES, RACES, AND CULTURES[1]

In tracing the problem of national minorities in the Union of Soviet Socialist Republics, Alfred G. Meyer described the society as multi-national in character. He saw the national minorities as not distributed evenly throughout the country. Rather, they are concentrated in various areas in the western and southern frontiers of the U.S.S.R., forming distinct national areas or regions. Counting every minor tribe, Soviet statistics in 1917 listed 182 separate nationalities speaking 149 different languages.

γ   γ   γ

Soviet society is a jumble of languages, races, and cultures. The task of making one nation out of them, or even of keeping this mixed society functioning, is complicated by the fact that the feelings of these various component peoples toward each other have not always been friendly. A long tradition of hostility, in fact, has sown suspicion between Georgians and Armenians, between Muslims and Jews. Some of the Soviet nations, especially in the Baltic and Transcaucasus areas, have in the past nursed feelings of superiority over the Russians, and hence a resentment at being ruled by them. Even where such feelings of superiority did not exist, the policies of discrimination and russification pursued by tsarist governments in the last decades before the revolution promoted resentment and hatred among Russia's national minorities. Once aroused, such feelings may linger on for decades and may today be factors still to reckon with. . . .

[1]Alfred G. Meyer, "The Problem of National Minorities in the USSR." In William J. Bossenbrook, ed., *Mid-Twentieth Century Nationalism* (Detroit, 1965), pp. 55–56, 68. By permission of Wayne State University Press.

What then is the total effect of Soviet nationality policies? Obviously, it too is ambiguous. Melting-pot trends in the direction of the development of a new Soviet nationality are matched by the intensification of national consciousness, if not among all the country's nationalities, then certainly among some of them. The differentiation and centrifugal tendencies resulting from this growth of national consciousness are sufficiently strong that in recent years even some high-ranking party leaders have wondered aloud whether national differences will disappear even under full-fledged communism.

Soviet nationality policy has at times been compared with colonialism because the regime's relation to its minorities has involved conquest, domination, and exploitation. Unlike most other colonial countries, however, Soviet rule has sought to bring its minority subjects into the twentieth century. It has acted as an agent of Western civilization. In the short run, this is likely to promote the development of national consciousness and thus further strain the fabric of Soviet society. If, in the long run, a new Soviet nationality emerges, the Soviet variant of colonialism may be of a self-liquidating kind.

READING NO. 18

THE UKRAINIAN NATIONAL REVIVAL[1]

The Ukrainian national revival reflected the truism that dangerous divisions exist in a multinational state over the course of centuries. In this article Paul Robert Magocsi, of the University of Toronto, traces the marked divisions that existed for many years among the peoples cast together in the modern Ukraine.

γ   γ   γ

The Ukrainians are considered to be but one other example of the many Slavic and other peoples in east-central Europe who experienced a national revival in the course of the nineteenth century. In comparative terms, the Ukrainian case is usually regarded as one that entered the national revival process relatively late, and that in the end it was not successful in fulfilling the ultimate goal of national movements—political independence. Such a perception—that national movements should be analyzed and implicitly judged by the degree to which they were or were not successful in obtaining political independence—has inevitably determined the philosophical and intellectual thrust of the literature on the subject. This study explores what, if any, framework or frameworks have been used in previous investigations to analyze the Ukrainian national revival, and it proposes a new one that will not only place the Ukrainian example in the larger European context, but will also respond to the specific characteristics of the Ukrainian experience.

By the time the earliest stages of the national awakening or revival had begun during the last decades of the eighteenth century, Ukrainian ethnolinguistic territory, that is, lands inhab-

[1]Paul Robert Magocsi, "The Ukrainian National Revival: A New Analytical Framework," *Canadian Review of Studies in Nationalism* Vol. XVI, No. 1–2, (1989), pp. 45–46, 57–58. By permission of the *Canadian Review of Studies in Nationalism*.

ited by Ukrainians, was located within the boundaries of two multinational empires—the Russian and the Austrian. This political division was to remain without substantial change until the end of World War I. From the standpoint of numbers, the Ukrainian lands within the Russian Empire were more important by far because 90% of all Ukrainian ethnolinguistic territory and 85% of all Ukrainian inhabitants resided there. On the other hand, despite the smaller percentages of land and people within the Austrian Empire, Ukrainians there, especially in the province of Galicia, were to play a significant if not decisive role in determining the direction of the Ukrainian national revival.

Within both empires, Ukrainians lacked any administrative unit that corresponded either in whole or in part to the lands they inhabited. Rather, they remained divided among the administrative units of these countries, neither of which recognized any specific Ukrainian territorial entity. Therefore, within the Russian Empire, Ukrainians lived primarily within nine *guberniia*, or provinces (Chernihiv, Poltava, Kharkiv, Kherson, Katerynoslav, Taurida, Volhynia, Kiev, and Podolia), which in whole or in part were sometimes loosely referred to as South Russia or Little Russia. Within the Austrian Empire, Ukrainians were to be found within parts of three areas: in the provinces (crownlands) of Galicia and Bukovina in the "Austrian half" of the empire, and in several counties of northeastern Hungary that were sometimes referred to as Subcarpathian Rus' (Ruthenia), later Transcarpathia.

Although by the nineteenth century Ukrainian lands enjoyed neither administrative unity nor autonomy, the inhabitants of certain regions, especially those descended from the Zaporozhian Cossacks, still had strong memories of self-rule. This was particularly the case in Ukrainian lands within the Russian Empire, three regions of which had enjoyed varying degrees of political autonomy until as late as the second half of the eighteenth century—the Sloboda Ukraine (to 1765), Zaporozhia (to 1775), and the Hetmanate (to 1785). . . .

If one assumes that the concepts of multiple hierarchy of loyalties and mutually-exclusive identities are both equally impartial aspects of Ukrainian historical development, then it might be useful, when analyzing the Ukrainian national revival, not to prejudge its intellectual leaders and the organizations they created solely on the degree to which they implicitly or explicitly contributed to the idea of national exclusivity. Therefore, when considering the whole course of the Ukrainian national revival, from the beginnings in the late eighteenth century through its culmination in World War I, as well as its evolution since then under Soviet rule, one would argue that the principle of a hierarchy of multiple loyalties, which assumes the existence of what social scientists call situational ethnicity, and which was evident during the nineteenth century within the Russian and Austrian Empires as well as more recently in the Soviet Union, is as "natural" a phenomenon in Ukrainian culture as the concept of mutually-exclusive identities that ostensibly can be promoted only with the attainment of independent statehood. . . .

READING NO. 19

ETHNOCENTRISM IN MOLDAVIA[1]

Although the Moldavian nationality wanted its own independence from Moscow, it was not about to tolerate any dissension in its own territory. James Carney, in a report to Time, *revealed this chaotic situation in one of the constituent republics of the Soviet Union.*

γ   γ   γ

A ragged band of 200 Moldavians, some armed with chains and knives, milled around the main square of rural Chimishliya last week waiting for orders to begin a civil war. "This is our land, our home, and we will fight for it," explained Ion Rosanu. "We have to protect the integrity of sovereign Moldavia." Rosanu and his companions were among thousands who mobilized to prevent the Gagauz, an ethnic Turkish minority, from seceding. When the Moldavians marched toward the Gagauz region, only the arrival of troops from the Soviet Interior Ministry kept the peace.

But the troops weren't enough to prevent bloodshed in the Dniester River valley, a region east of the Moldavian capital of Kishinev where ethnic Russians have also proclaimed their independence from the republic. Skirmishes between Moldavians and Russians outside the town of Dubossary reportedly left at least six dead and 30 wounded.

Appealing for peace, Gorbachev seemed to take sides with the Moldavians, saying, "We have to give separatists a real fight here." But the violence showed just how tenuous a hold the Kremlin has on its splintering empire. As ethnocentrism sweeps through the land, even minorities as small as the 150,000-strong Gagauz are seeking self-rule. And Russians, who once enjoyed colonial privileges in the outlying Soviet republics, now find themselves on the defensive as nationalism prevails.

---

[1]*Time*, November 12, 1990, p. 46. Copyright 1990. The Time Inc. Magazine Company. Reprinted by permission.

READING NO. 20

SOVIET TATARS DEMAND INDEPENDENCE FROM THE RUSSIAN REPUBLIC[1]

No sooner did the Russian Soviet Federated Socialist Republic declare its sovereignty than it had to face challenges inside its own territory. Soviet Tatars inside the large Russian Republic wanted independence of their own. It was a chaotic situation as more and more ethnic groups demanded satisfaction for their own brand of nationalism. Newsweek *correspondent Carroll Bogert described the situation.*

γ   γ   γ

For Lithuanians, Georgians and others trying to break away from the Soviet Union, it may seem hard to believe. But there's actually one place that's trying to *become* a Soviet republic. The former "autonomous" republic of Tataria, 460 miles due east of Moscow, was part of the Russian Republic until Aug. 30. Then, at the goading of Tatar nationalists, the local parliament unanimously changed the region's name to Tatarstan, declared its laws supreme over those of Russia and claimed its natural resources on behalf of its 3.7 million people. "We want to be on that list of members of the Soviet Union. And in alphabetical order—ahead of the Ukraine," says Vladimir Yermakov, an aide to Tatarstan's Supreme Soviet chairman, Mintimir Shaimeyev. . . .

The local Communist Party leadership may have hoped to dampen nationalist fervor by proclaiming sovereignty. The effect appears to have been just the opposite. Tatar groups are now pressing for more Tatar-speaking schools, Islamic education and days off on the Muslim holy Friday instead of Sunday. They hope to activate the millions of Tatars living outside the republic to make the Tatar nation great again.

READING NO. 21

THE COURSE OF GERMAN NATIONALISM TO WORLD WAR I[1]

German nationalism, from its early romantic stage to the collapse in 1918, had severe repercussions for the German people. The steady exaggeration of national pride and the exercise of the wrong kind of nationalism led to disastrous results.

γ   γ   γ

1. In so far as "national character" can be said to exist, the German form was generated environmentally in the Prusso-German symbiosis. The quality of German nationalism took on such Prussian characteristics as State-worship, emphasis upon discipline and obedience, veneration for the leader, the power-culture synthesis or dualism, militarism, and the promulgation of a world-mission.

2. In the fields of pedagogy and education, vital in the genesis and development of the sentiment of nationalism, the aims and methods of the Prusso-German educational system remained until 1945 as nationalistically oriented as they were originally projected by *Turnvater* Jahn.

3. The conception of the Grimm brothers that all their works relate to the Fatherland, "from whose soil they derive their strength," applies even to the *Fairy Tales*, which, hitherto, have been considered as universalist in character. German literature in general reflected the quality of the steadily increasing strength of nationalism.

4. Concurrent with Prussia's drive for political hegemony was a parallel and successful appropriation of economic power. In a most important step in the economic unification of Ger-

[1] Based on Louis L. Snyder, *German Nationalism: The Tragedy of a People* (Harrisburg, Pa., 1952) and Port Washington, N.Y. 1969), pp. 306–309. Courtesy of The Stackpole Co., Inc.

many, leadership of the *Zollverein*, originally the brain-child of the Württemberger economist, Friedrich List, was assumed by Prussia.

5. The Western type of liberalism, stemming out of the Enlightenment, with its accent upon the individual before the State, was bypassed in the Germanies in favor of Prussian liberalism, with its glorification of the State above the individual. The Revolution of 1848 in the Germanies marked the vaporization of Western liberalism, the triumph of the Prussian version, and the preëminence of nationalism. The process was extended in Bismarck's policy of *Blut-und-Eisen* and the three wars of national unification.

6. German historiography from Justus Möser to Heinrich von Treitschke helped to shape German history by opposing Germany to the West. There was a close connection between the intellectual aims of German historians and the doctrinaire political philosophy of the practical men of affairs who were in a position to implement nationalist ideology.

7. The direction and quality of extremist nationalism were heralded in the cultural extremism of Richard Wagner, the fanatical anti-Semitism of Court-Pastor Adolf Stoecker, and the pseudo-philosophical irrationalism of Julius Langbehn, Arthur de Gobineau, Houston Stewart Chamberlain, and Oswald Spengler.

8. While it existed in every important country, war-cult extremism in Germany from Karl von Clausewitz to Ewald Banse took on an extraordinary intensity.

9. The framework of Prusso-German nationalism was so rigid that even liberals like Friedrich Meinecke, despite high personal integrity and tortuous self-examination, were caught in the straight jacket.

10. The historical roots of German nationalism were so strong that not even the defeat of World War I was decisive enough to destroy them.

There is a dichotomy between extremism and liberalism in the development of German nationalism. That much more attention has been devoted to extremist strands in the pattern may be attributed to the fact that liberalism as understood in the Western sense was weak and ineffective in Germany. The climate of opinion in Germany over decades was extremist in character. Germany was plagued by the wrong kind of nationalism. Intellectual theorists, political leaders, and demagogues in Germany were entranced by the notion of power. This idea existed elsewhere, but in Germany the concept of *Macht* took on special meaning. The German people contributed much to Western civilization, but their overemphasis upon power was to bring them unexpected misfortune.

READING NO. 22

BISMARCK'S "IRON-AND-BLOOD" SPEECH, SEPTEMBER 30, 1862[1]

On September 30, 1862, Bismarck appeared before the Budget Commission of the Lower House of the Prussian Parliament and attempted to persuade it to appropriate increased funds for the army desired by William I. One phase from this speech, with its rhythm changed from "iron and blood" to "blood and iron," contributed to a significant change in the nature of German nationalism.

γ   γ   γ

Germany looks not to Prussia's liberalism but to her power. Bavaria, Württemberg, and Baden may indulge in liberalism, but no person will because of that reason assign Prussia's role to them. Prussia must gather up her strength and maintain it in readiness for the opportune moment, which already has passed by several times. Since the Treaty of Vienna, Prussia's borders have not been favorable for a healthy state life. Not by parliamentary speeches and majority votes are the great questions of the day determined—that was the great mistake of 1848 and 1849—but by iron and blood.

---

[1]Quoted in J. Hohfeld, *Deutsche Reichsgeschichte in Dokumenten* (Berlin, 1927), p. 27. Translated by the editor.

READING NO. 23

GERMAN NATIONALISM IN 1914[1]

German nationalism at the outbreak of World War I encompassed all elements of the population. The drive for "a place in the sun" was widely supported. When the war began, 93 prominent German intellectuals issued a manifesto signed by some of the most respected individuals in the country. It reflected wide national support for Wilhelm II in the war against the Allies.

γ   γ   γ

TO THE CIVILIZED WORLD! As representatives of German Science and Art, we hereby protest to the civilized world against the lies and calumnies with which our enemies are endeavoring to stain the honor of Germany in her hard struggle for existence—in a struggle that has been forced on her.

The iron mouth of events has proved the untruth of the fictitious German defeats; consequently misrepresentation and calumny are all the more eagerly at work. As heralds of truth we raise our voices against these.

It is not true that Germany is guilty of having caused this war. Neither the people, the Government, nor the "Kaiser" wanted war. . . .

It is not true that we trespassed in neutral Belgium. It has been proved that France and England had resolved on such a trespass, and it has likewise been proved that Belgium had agreed to their doing so. It would have been suicide on our part not to have been beforehand.

---

[1]A. Morel-Fatio, *Les Versions allemande et française du manifeste dit des intellectuels allemands dit des quatre-vingt-treize*, as quoted in R. H. Lutz, *Fall of the German Empire* (Stanford University, California, 1932) I, 74–78.

It is not true that the life and property of a single Belgian citizen was injured by our soldiers without the bitterest defense having made it necessary. . . .

It is not true that our troops treated Louvain brutally. Furious inhabitants having treacherously fallen upon them in their quarters, our troops with aching hearts were obliged to fire a part of the town, as punishment. The greatest part of Louvain has been preserved. . . .

It is not true that our warfare pays no respects to international laws. It knows no undisciplined cruelty. But in the east, the earth is saturated with the blood of women and children unmercifully butchered by the wild Russian troops, and in the west, dumdum bullets mutilate the breasts of our soldiers. . . .

It is not true that the combat against our so-called militarism is not a combat against our civilization, as our enemies hypocritically pretend it is. Were it not for German militarism, German civilization would long since have been extirpated. . . .

We cannot wrest the poisonous weapon—the lie—out of the hands of our enemies. All we can do is proclaim to all the world, that our enemies are giving false witness against us. . . .

Have faith in us! Believe, that we shall carry on this war to the end as a civilized nation, to whom the legacy of a Goethe, a Beethoven, and a Kant, is just as sacred as its own hearths and homes.

> EMIL VON BEHRING, Professor of Medicine, Marburg
> Prof. PAUL EHRLICH, Frankfort on the Main
> FRITZ HABER, Professor of Chemistry, Berlin
> ERNST HAECKEL, Professor of Zoology, Jena
> Prof. ADOLF VON HARNACK, General Director of the Royal Library, Berlin
> KARL LAMPRECHT, Professor of History, Leipzig
> MAX LIEBERMAN, Berlin
> MAX PLANCK, Professor of Physics, Berlin
> Prof. MAX REINHARDT, Director of the German Theatre, Berlin
> WILHELM RÖNTGEN, Professor of Physics, Munich
> GUSTAV VON SCHMOLLER, Professor of National Economy,
>
> . . . .

READING NO. 24

SOVIET COMMUNISM COMES CRASHING DOWN[1]

Soviet communism came into existence in 1917 with a successful revolution. It ended with a coup that failed in an upsurge of democratic sentiment. The Russian people, condemned to more than seven decades of a servile status, rose in rebellion and put an end to communism.

γ   γ   γ

Tyranny is most vulnerable when it tries to reform. For seven decades, the Soviet Union preserved itself entirely by force. Lenin used it implacably. Stalin was even more ruthless; he killed perhaps 20 million of his own people, and for most of his long reign, his control was never threatened. Nikita Khrushchev loosened the chains a bit, and hard-liners deposed him for "hare-brained schemes." When years of stagnation made change a do-or-die necessity, Mikhail Gorbachev tried to save the Soviet system by making it more humane and more efficient. But the forces of reform soon got out of hand and overwhelmed him, bringing down both the party and the state.

"We're now living in a new world," Gorbachev said forlornly last week as he finally announced his decision to "discontinue my activities" as Soviet president. The union did not outlast him by long. The next day a remnant of the country's first freely elected legislature held a sad little meeting and pronounced itself dead. The Soviet regime passed into history at the age of 74, unmourned by millions of survivors, who were more absorbed with building new nations—or finding something to eat.

The collapse was so swift and complete that some Westerners may wonder now why the Soviet Union obsessed and frightened

---

[1]*Newsweek*, January 6, 1992, pp. 12–15. Courtesy of *Newsweek*.

them for decades. Could Moscow ever have been the expansionist menace that inspired so much cold-war defense spending and
so many bomb shelters and set off so many political and military
confrontations? The perception that worldwide communism was
a monolithic and perhaps unstoppable force turned out to be
mistaken. Khrushchev's boast—"We will bury you"—has
been neatly reversed. But any regime that could sacrifice its own
people by the millions had to be considered lethally dangerous
to others. The West stood up to the challenge. Containment, the
strategy articulated by George Kennan in 1947, worked in the
end.

Yet the fall of the Soviet state struck few notes of triumph
overseas. "Democracy has prevailed in its worldwide struggle
against tyranny; why are democrats not dancing in the streets?"
asked conservative columnist William Safire. Perhaps it was
because Gorbachev gave up the ghost on Christmas Day, while
many Westerners were distracted. Perhaps it was because the
Soviet collapse had been anticipated for so long, and its consequences were soberingly difficult to control or even to predict.
Or perhaps there was a realization that the failure of Soviet
communism was not necessarily a victory for multiparty democracy and free enterprise, alien ideas that have not yet taken
deep root in the frozen soil of the newborn Commonwealth of
Independent States.

The system invented by Lenin and Stalin was destroyed by its
own inner contradictions—as Marxist theorists might say in
some other context. The state depended for its existence on
total, centralized political and economic control by the Soviet
Communist Party. But that leaden hand eventually produced a
country that was simply too backward to compete with the rest
of the world and too weak politically to hang onto its empire in
Eastern Europe. The result was a crisis of self-confidence in
Soviet Communism. The controls had to be relaxed. Dictatorship
turned wimpish, and reform quickly made tyranny untenable.

The Soviet system was an epochal social experiment that
captured the imagination of half the world while it appalled and
frightened the other half. On the ruins of autocracy, world war,
and civil strife, it built a new society based on the principle of
equality and the abolition of private property. "I have been over
into the future, and it works," radical American journalist

Lincoln Steffens wrote in 1931, after a visit to the Soviet Union. Marshaling raw resources, both human and material, the Soviet state built a huge industrial base. Despite vast suffering, it summoned up the fighting spirit to defeat the Nazi juggernaut. It produced stunning scientific achievements: a Soviet atomic bomb in 1949, sputnik in 1957, Yuri Gagarin's first manned spaceflight in 1961. "Whether you like it or not, history is on our side," Khrushchev bragged in 1956.

From almost the beginning, however, the Soviet system betrayed its own ideals in the most violent and sordid ways. Beginning in 1929, Stalin reintroduced a kind of serfdom when he forced most of the country's peasants onto collective farms. When the peasants resisted, millions of the more prosperous farmers, known pejoratively as kulaks, were stripped of their property and exiled to Siberia. Then the state wiped out lingering defiance through a deliberate "terror famine" in 1932. All told, as many as 11 million people died during collectivization. Millions more perished in Stalin's great purges in the late 1930s, when the dictator's critics and opponents—real or imaged— were marked for extermination or disappearance into the gulag. "A single death is a tragedy, a million deaths is a statistic," Stalin was quoted as saying. His crimes were denounced by Khrushchev in 1956 and later, more effectively, by Gorbachev. But the sycophants who survived the purges furnished the presiding deadwood for Leonid Brezhnev's regime.

Western socialists began to turn against Soviet communism as early as the 1930s, when Stalin's show trials made gorges rise. By Brezhnev's heyday, genuine belief in communism had all but died out in the Soviet Union itself. It was replaced by bitter cynicism and by a deadly form of egalitarianism that unconsciously prefers shared misery to individual advancement. Rigid central authority was stifling the economy and papering over the ethnic conflicts that would eventually help tear the country apart. A gigantic military buildup—prompted by Khrushchev's humiliation in the Cuban missile crisis of 1962—was impoverishing the nation. After successful interventions in a number of "fraternal socialist" countries, including Hungary in 1956 and Czechoslovakia in 1968, the Kremlin went one bridge too far and tried to subdue unruly Afghanistan, miring itself in a rocky quagmire.

That set the stage for Gorbachev's rise to power in 1985 and the well-meaning reforms that within a few years would destroy the system rather than save it. "He didn't know how to make sausage, but he did know how to provide freedom," the daily Komsomolskaya Pravda said of Gorbachev, not unkindly. But for the moment, at least, most citizens of the former Soviet Union were more concerned with obtaining sausages than freedom. Gorbachev himself insisted that his policies were "historically correct," though he admitted to "certain mistakes and blunders" in execution. He said he would remain in politics somehow—"I have big plans," he told reporters enigmatically—and he warned President Bush: "Watch out for Russia. They will zig and zag. It won't all be straightforward."

The principal successor to eight Soviet leaders is Russian President Boris Yeltsin, who gave up on the Communist Party only in 1990, after it gave up on him. Yeltsin thwarted the communists' final use of force during the coup last August. "We are sick and tired of pessimism," he said the day Gorbachev quit. "The people . . . need some faith, finally." It has been decades since the Soviet Union gave its own people something worthy of their faith, if it ever did. Rebuilding their hope may be Yeltsin's toughest challenge.

READING NO. 25

A. J. P. TAYLOR ON
THE GERMAN NATIONAL CHARACTER[1]

*A. J. P. Taylor (1906–1990), British historian and journalist, was
an iconoclastic scholar whose books infuriated professional
academic historians. His best-known book,* The Origins of
World War II, *was denounced by his colleague at Oxford
University, Hugh Trevor-Roper, who found Taylor's book just
about wrong in every respect. Taylor's controversial thesis was
that Hitler had not been solely responsible for the war, a view
widely at variance with standard interpretations. British historian A. L. Rowse described the book as "flawed from top to
bottom and offers an extraordinary instance of how history
should not be written." However, many historians were impressed with Taylor's view of German national character until 1945.*

γ   γ   γ

The history of the Germans is a history of extremes. It
contains everything except moderation, and in the course of a
thousand years the Germans have experienced everything except normality. They have dominated Europe, and they have
been the helpless victims of the domination of others; they have
enjoyed liberties unparalleled in Europe and they have fallen
victims to despotisms equally without parallel; they have produced the most transcendental philosophers, the most spiritual
musicians, and the most ruthless and unscrupulous politicians.
'German' has meant at one moment a being so sentimental, so
trusting; so pious, as to be too good for this world; and at
another a being so brutal, so unprincipled, so degraded, as to be
not fit to live. Both descriptions are true; both types of Germans
have existed not only at the same epoch, but in the same person.

[1]A. J. P. Taylor, *The Course of German History: A Survey of the Development of
Germany Since 1815* (London, 1945), p. 1. Courtesy of H. Hamilton, Publisher.

Only the normal person, not particularly good, not particularly bad, healthy, sane, moderate—he has never set his stamp on German history. Geographically the people of the center, the Germans have never found a middle way of life, either in their thought or least of all in their politics. One looks in vain in their history for a *juste milieu*, for common sense—the two qualities which have distinguished France and England. Nothing is normal in German history except violent oscillations.

READING NO. 26

POLICY STATEMENT OF
HANS-DIETRICH GENSCHER ON
THE REUNIFICATION OF GERMANY[1]

On September 20, 1990, Hans-Dietrich Genscher, Minister for Foreign Affairs of the Federal Republic of West Germany, issued a policy statement regarding the reunification of Germany. He expressed his thanks to the West: "As we approach German unity, we Germans would like to thank our friends and allies in the West for paving the way for our reintegration into the community of free nations."

γ　　　　　　γ　　　　　　γ

On October 3 the German people will once again be living in one democratic state—for the first time in 57 years. We are looking forward to that day with joy and gratitude. It is an occasion for reflection.

After January 30, 1933, when the darkness of fascism descended on Germany, we lost first our freedom and our internal peace. We lost our external peace and we lost our national unity.

Many Germans lost their life and their health, their possessions and their homeland. And we all lost the respect and friendship of other nations. All that began on January 30, 1933. Conscious of the four powers' approval of our national unity, we commemorate the untold suffering brought on other nations in the name of Germany. We commemorate the victims of the war and totalitarianism.

We are united in the intention never to allow any of this to happen again. Our thoughts turn especially to the Jewish people. The united German, too, will be aware of its special responsibility towards the Jewish people.

[1]German Information Center, Vol. XIII, No. 18, September 26, 1990.

In discussing today the signing of the treaty on the final settlement we are aware that the family of nations accompany us with their trust on the way to national unity. The establishment of a political and social order based on freedom in the Federal Republic of Germany, and our country's policy of peace and responsibility, has won us back the trust of the nations.

The peaceful revolution for freedom in the German Democratic Republic convinced the nations of the world that the Germans are using the opportunity of freedom to strengthen freedom and peace. The world has recognized that we Germans are banking on the peace-enhancing strength of human rights and dignity, of freedom and democracy.

The united Germany will be open to the world, thus doing justice to its greater responsibility in this respect as well. The more our national and social order is based on freedom, tolerance, justice and social responsibility, the more we will be able to win the confidence of other nations, and the more we will be acting in accordance with the basic values enshrined in our constitution and the spirit of the peaceful revolution in the GDR. Particularly at this time, freedom, tolerance, justice and social responsibility, solidarity and fraternity will have to stand the test in the German unification process.

READING NO. 27

GERMANS JOYOUSLY GREET
THEIR NEW REUNIFICATION[1]

Stripped of the kind of aggressive nationalism that had brought them misery and despair in two World Wars, Germans in early October 1990 celebrated their unity in a pensive key. Craig R. Whitney, reporting for The New York Times, *described their rejoicing mitigated by undercurrents of struggle and doubt.*

γ   γ   γ

BERLIN, Oct. 3—Germans, whether they had lived in East Germany or West Germany, woke up this morning in Germany, a country nobody had known since the end of World War II.

In a way, after the fall of the Berlin wall and the rest of the Iron Curtain last year, the events seemed anticlimactic, though they set the formal seal on the end of the cold war and brought an end to the division of Europe that began with Yalta and Potsdam.

But the division really began with Hitler and the war he launched in 1939, as President Richard von Weizsäcker reminded Germans in a speech today on the day of unity, a glorious day of warm, summer-like sunshine and golden autumn leaves. His was one of many appeals to Germans today to be "nachdenklich," a word meaning reflective, meditative and subdued that seemed to capture the national mood.

Germany's Western allies had reason to feel the same way today, as unification marked the formal end of the long cold war. By the logic of that struggle, West Germany had devoted itself to democratic political and military integration with the West. . . .

The atmosphere in Bach's St. Thomas Church [in Leipzig], on the eve of unification, spoke eloquently. Inside, visitors from

[1]Craig R. Whitney, in *The New York Times*, October 4, 1990. Copyright © by The New York Times Company. Reprinted by permission.

171

all over Europe had posted a whole bulletin board with prayers that things would turn out better this time than they had the last time Germany was united.

One, from a German man from Düsseldorf, said: "God give the German people an understanding of their past mistakes. It must not happen again."

On the organ, a Bach chorale-prelude on the hymn "Now Thank We All Our God" echoed through the sober Gothic nave, the cantus firmus melody seeming to speak through the plaintive minor-key accompaniment of struggle and doubt, rather than thanksgiving.

READING NO. 28

EUROPEANS ACCEPT GERMAN REUNIFICATION[1]

Umberto Eco, a professor of Semiotics at the University of Bologna and a successful Italian writer, expressed a sentiment widely held in 1990 by many observers. "I do not fear German nationalism."

γ   γ   γ

It is an unavoidable process because a country with one tradition and one language has the right to find unity for itself. Nothing can stop such a natural trend. We have to respect this natural urge, this tendency to be a single nation.

Germany has a similar history to Italy's.

If you look at the historical background of Germany you see almost a neurotic split personality. On one side there is a nationalistic, imperialistic Prussian drive. On the other hand, there is a part of German culture that is constantly critical of itself, much like Italians are. The Italian national sport is self-criticism. There is a struggle between the two sides of the German soul. But there are two of them.

I cannot say that a country or a culture is condemned to behave always in the same way. To think that is another form of racism.

In the last century both tried to establish themselves as separate countries. I understand the worries of other European countries. But I don't have that typical concern—the fear of a new pan-Germany, the fear of a new Nazism—because the younger generation is different from the previous one and democracy has produced a profound change.

---

[1]*The New York Times*, September 27, 1990. Copyright © by The New York Times Company. Reprinted by permission.

When I meet German people of my generation I find people who have a sense of their historical responsibility for what Nazism had been. They have a profound sense of what their duty should be. I do not fear German nationalism.

READING NO. 29

LORD SHAWCROSS ON
THE NEW GERMANY[1]

*Lord Shawcross, British jurist and former Labor Party politi-
cian, served as Britain's Attorney-General from 1945 to 1951.
After World War II he was chief British prosecutor at the
Nuremberg trials. He favored German reunification but warned
that the Germans might one day use their new political power
commensurate with their economic prosperity.*

γ   γ   γ

I think the Nuremberg trial was useful, particularly, in that it
rehearsed the history of the war, and of the events leading up to
it, in a way that might never had been done, otherwise, or would
have taken many years. Because the Germans had in their
methodical way kept nearly all the historical documents, instead
of destroying them, and because the Americans had processed
them efficiently, the case against the Nazi war criminals was
almost entirely made by documents. It didn't have to rely on
witnesses. Because of this documentation, the German people
accepted the fact that the Nazi leadership had been an evil
regime. They are a very different people to what we thought
during the war.

[1]*The New York Times*, September 27, 1990. Copyright © by The New York
Times Company. Reprinted by permission.

READING NO. 30

AMERICANS EXPRESS SUPPORT BUT ADVISE CAUTION[1]

Americans in general supported the unification of the two Germanys. At the same time, experts on German history believed it best, in view of Germany's past history, to be cautious about a revival of German nationalism. Gordon A. Craig, dean of American scholars on German history, stated in an interview that the Germans had changed, but also that unification might change them again.

γ   γ   γ

Professor Craig said he had been disquieted by some elements of "triumphalism" in the recent speeches of Chancellor Helmut Kohl, in the behavior of West German soccer fans. "But nothing compared to 1871," he said.

"The West German republic is a success story," he continued. "Its crises were overcome pretty well by democratic procedures. There is grass-roots democracy there. On the whole I'm very optimistic about it. I keep telling myself that the Germans have changed and that it cannot be reversed. But then I remind myself that unification will change them again."

[1]*The New York Times*, September 28, 1990. Copyright © by The New York Times Company. Reprinted by permission.

READING NO. 31

WILLIAM L. SHIRER ON THE GERMANS AS A PEOPLE OF EXTREMES[1]

William L. Shirer, distinguished journalist of World War II and author of The Rise and Fall of the Third Reich, *remained skeptical. He held that, considering the past history of Germany, there was room to believe that nationalism might well engulf the German people after unification.*

γ   γ   γ

"It makes me very uneasy," Shirer said of the unification of Germany. "partly because of past history. Twice in my own lifetime they have gone against most of the rest of the world."

"It's 40 years," he continued. "Maybe it's time enough for a great people to change their characteristics. But we just don't know. You have to be careful not to indict a whole people, but they are a people of extremes."

"The Germans I met first in Paris were liberal or Socialist, democratic and open, tolerant," he said. "Years later, I looked them up in Berlin and they had gotten the bug," he said, of the ideology of Nazism.

"The thing that shocked me was this horrible, barbaric movement and that most of the decent Germans joined in," he said. "The whole damned society supported it."

The author was last in Germany in 1985 and he said: "My impression was that their devotion to ideology had become very thin. They were interested in creature comforts and nice vacations."

That idea, said Mr. Shirer, consoled him as he contemplated German unification.

[1]*The New York Times*, September 28, 1990. Copyright © by The New York Times Company. Reprinted by permission.

READING NO. 32

STATUS OF THE MINI-NATIONALISMS[1]

The existence of the mini-nationalisms and their threat to the centralized nationalism of the current nation-states was treated in this excerpt from the Encyclopedia of Nationalism. *It shows how the complicated structure of nation-states in the contemporary world has been threatened by those ethnic groups seeking a nationalism of their own.*

γ   γ   γ

MINI-NATIONALISMS. Under political control of larger nationalisms, mini-nationalisms are supported by those dissatisfied peoples who want either more autonomy inside the structure of the national state or demand independence. They are sometimes identified as regionalisms, separatisms, or ethnic groups. The people belonging to a mini-nationalism generally see themselves as bound together by history, traditions, customs, language, perhaps religion, and believe themselves to have been incorporated unjustly into the territory of a more powerful state. People of moderate bent are willing to remain under the political control of those they regard as foreigners, provided they are given a measure of autonomy, the power or right of a certain amount of self-government. The people of Wales and Scotland take this moderate position. There are also those of revolutionary zeal who see their status as completely unfair and unreasonable and who opt for independence. Where the moderates turn to negotiation, the radicals choose bullets and bombs to enforce their demands. The Basques in Spain and the Croats in Yugoslavia are examples of the mini-nationalists who seek freedom from the centralized state by the use of extremist force.

[1]From Louis L. Snyder, *Encyclopedia of Nationalism* (New York, 1990), pp. 212–214. Courtesy of Paragon Press.

The political units that are called modern states are held together by the cement of nationalism, which has many faces. As national states were formed in the modern era, the drive for unification almost invariably brought diverse peoples together in a nationalist mold. These were often peoples of different languages and varied cultures. They were required to accept the domination of a central authority, and they were expected to endure assimilation designed to strengthen the central authority. This was one vital trend in the construction of a larger national- ism. Added to it was a reverse movement toward disruption as the mini-nationalism emerged to demand its own special rights. These dissatisfied groups, holding a developing nationalism of their own, were banded into the framework of the national state. They either accepted their status or began to agitate for their own smaller nationalism.

Thus, a mini-nationalism is a little nationalism under the control of a larger nationalism. It is the sentiment of a people who see themselves as distinct and would prefer their own state or union with another state that they regard as having a similar history. They see themselves as held in bondage by "foreigners" against their will. They point to their own historical, linguistic, cultural, religious, and psychological ties, and believe that they are, in a combination of several of these factors, different enough to warrant emancipation from the larger nationalism. In other words, a mini-nationalism may be regarded as a national- ism that has not yet come of age. In this sense, a small or a substantially large minority inside the existing state may seek the status of a separate state. It may call for freedom from an "alien nationalism" and for the territory that it believes to be necessary for the formation of a new and independent national state.

For an already established national state composed of many different nationalities, the call by mini-nationalists for freedom presents a problem of critical importance. For example, the Soviet Union, with its multiple nationalities, regarded the effort to obtain freedom as simple treason. For the Kremlin, one successful mini-nationalism would result in the domino-like effect leading to the dismemberment of the national state. For that reason until recently, the Armenians, or Latvians, Lithua- nians, and Estonians were held rigidly to the central authority and allowed little autonomy and certainly no independence. In recent years there has been an upsurge in the demand of such mini-nationalisms for independence.

Mini-nationalisms come into existence when a small group of local patriots begin to see themselves as a distinct nationality. They regard themselves as liberators, who point to the past of their people as reason enough to make demands on the central state. They hammer away at the claim that their linguistic aspirations have been denied in an alien society. They would have their own nation with its distinctive flag and their own national anthem. They denounce their fellow citizens as mired in apathy, indifference, or too mild support. They see themselves as chosen by destiny to lead their people out of enforced subjugation. If the process seems too slow, they turn to violence in the belief that assassinations and bombings are much more effective than words in the struggle for independence.

Thus, for the extreme mini-nationalist, the power principle is all important. He regards being controlled by a centralized authority as a violation of his rights, and he is determined to push his claims to the limit. He knows that there is no outside force able to mediate between centralization and decentralization, between state authority and dissatisfied regionalists. He believes that any effort by such an organization as the United Nations would be deemed as interference in the internal affairs of a sovereign state. Therefore, he uses the force of his own followers to achieve what he believes to be in the best interests of his people.

Mini-nationalisms may vary in type. National minorities in older nations may feel that they have been left behind in the nation-making process (Scots in Britain, Armenians in the Soviet Union). Others may be dissatisfied in several nations and struggle for early independence (Kurds in Iraq, Iran, and Turkey). There may be unfulfilled communities that see themselves as vestiges of an independence movement or they may be separatists who want to be another nation (Quebecers in Canada). All such varying types want their aspirations to be recognized.

The phenomenon is global. In both the established nations and in new nations, minorities have been forced into subjugation. Following the collapse of great empires after World War I and World War II, dozens of new nations emerged. An upsurge of nationalism was to be expected as these new nations were consolidated and formed their own governments. There was no set pattern in this development: new boundaries were fixed with little or no regard for the diverse peoples inside them. Africans and Asians who had learned nationalism from their former suppressors, began to form their own process of territorialization. They put peoples of differing backgrounds together as they fashioned their national states. This was by no means a diffusion from European experience, but it was actually political parallelism.

To establish states, mini-nationalisms present a danger. Propaganda by separatist factions, far from diminishing in recent years, has increased. Separatists usually work inside the larger state, but there has begun a wide international movement. French historian Charles Seignobos suggested "a syndicate of little discontented nations," which would be set up in Paris. Eventually, several European mini-nationalists established in 1975 a small bureau with headquarters in Brussels. Whether or not this organization intended to handle the claims of regionalists as well as small nations is not altogether clear. In any event, its work has been ineffective. Disaffected small nationalisms remain everywhere throughout the world, from Sri Lanka to Spain.

READING NO. 33

YUGOSLAVIA'S ETHNIC GROUPS
CALL FOR SELF-DETERMINATION[1]

*The disintegration of the Yugoslav state seemed inevitable as the
Serbo-Croat relationship moved into the critical phase. The
decentralization of power among the six constituent republics
and the two provinces had made the country virtually ungovernable. A German observer, Harry Schleicher, comments on the
incompatibilities in a multinational state.*

γ   γ   γ

The multinational state of Yugoslavia is reeling from one
nationality conflict into another. New and apparently incurable
wounds have been added to the trouble spot of Kosovo, with its
rapidly increasing Albanian majority population.

Slovenia, the most economically developed of the six constituent republics and once one of the mainstays of the state
founded in 1918, is striving for independence. This inevitably
leads to a disastrous reactivation of the Serbo-Croat relationship
which is so decisive for the existence of the Yugoslavian state as
a whole.

It is pointless asking why this development has come about.
Perhaps the state which was composed of peoples with such
different characters was a miscarriage right from the start. The
incompatibilities, which were often fostered to the point of open
hostility, became clear in the period between the two world
wars. During world war two they continued in a bloodbath.

National passions, however, were hardly purged by this
bloodshed. The motto "Brotherliness and Unity" put out by
Tito's victorious partisans could only be sustained as long as the
Communists had the country firmly under control.

[1]Harry Schleicher, in the *Kölner Stadt-Anzeiger*, October 11, 1990, translated in
The German Tribune, October 21, 1990, p. 2. Courtesy of *The German Tribune*.

The decline of Communism in Eastern Europe has also opened up many a floodgate in the Yugoslavian multinational state. The decentralisation of power in favour of the six constituent republics, which was introduced during Tito's lifetime, has made Yugoslavia virtually ungovernable.

The complicated 1974 constitution, which was designed to foster the balance of national interests, is now being more or less deliberately ignored by political leaders in the six republics. Yugoslavia no longer exists in the form established after the war. If there were a political divorce law it would have long since formally disintegrated.

In the meantime, other options are being considered. A plan presented by Slovenia and Croatia, to turn the crumbling federal state into a confederation of states, would mean a *de facto* division. However, the idea that six constituent republics with separate armies, separate currencies and an independent foreign policy would form a workable community of interests does seem to be wishful thinking.

It remains to be seen which alternative proposals are made by the Yugoslavian presidium of state. One thing is clear: Serbia, the largest and most populous republic, does not think much of the idea of a confederation. It's President, Slobódan Milosevic, who is a controversial figure in non-Serbian parts of the republic, announced that Serbia would either remain in the federal state or would organise itself as an independent state.

The disintegration of the Yugoslavian state seems inevitable. Even assuming the goodwill of all parties concerned, a divorce in mutual agreement would be political masterpiece. The aim is not only to distribute the "family silver," which in Yugoslavia's case, admittedly, consists of international liabilities more than anything else.

The main problem are "the children:" in other words, the cross-border national minorities. Bosnia and Herzegovina, for example, where there is relatively little unrest, is a classic example of a Balkan nationality patchwork rug which cannot be untied.

If Yugoslavia is dissolved as a federal state, Serbia intends demarcating new inner-Yugoslavian borders and 'fetching home' as many fellow Serbs as possible. Such concepts threaten to provoke even more dramatic conflicts. The violence exhibited in the "autonomy" unilaterally declared by the Serb minority in Croatia is a foretaste.

Unfortunately, the solution to the multi-nationality problem is not facilitated by the process of democratisation. Fears seem justified that Yugoslavia—apart from the Soviet Union—will soon become Europe's problem country.

READING NO. 34

DISSENTING NATIONALISM SWEEPS OVER CROATIA[1]

Violence by extreme Croatian nationalists had behind it a long history of intellectual dissent. Konstantin Symmons-Symonolewicz described the powerful impulse toward Croatian romantic nationalism in the early nineteenth century. This explains the reluctance of Croatians to be included in the contemporary Yugoslavian state.

γ   γ   γ

In Croatia, the beginnings of what was to be called *Preporod* (that is, national "revival") were associated with the reincorporation into the country of those districts that for a few years (1808–1815) had been a part of the so-called Illyrian Provinces, set up by Napoleon. This brought into Croatia a whole army of young men who under the French regime had become inspired by a very strong romantic nationalism, infused with advanced social doctrines, and impatient of any idea of Croatia's subordination to Hungary. This new nationalism, says C. A. Macartney, swept over Croatia like a heath fire, setting students and young 'intellectuals' aflame, throwing out fiery streams of grammarians, lexicographers, poets and political journalists, and penetrating even the aristocracy. The Croat nobles, who had hitherto shown little interest in their native language, identified themselves enthusiastically with the young nationalist movement. In 1832, the Croat magnate Baron Rukovina addressed the Sabor (the National Assembly) in Croat, a language which it had not heard for centuries. In 1833, Count Janko Draskovic—an elderly man, a Court Chamberlain, a member of the House of

[1]Konstantin Symmons-Symonolewicz, *Nationalist Movements: A Comparative View* (Meadville, Pa., 1970), p. 26. Reprinted by permisson of Maplewood Press.

Magnates, and a Colonel—published a pamphlet containing a complete political program for the constitution of Croatia, with other provinces of the Habsburg empire inhabited by the Southern Slavs, as a separate political unit.

READING NO. 35

THE CROATIAN NATIONAL CONGRESS DENOUNCES MARSHAL TITO[1]

Croatian dissidents abroad waged a bitter campaign against Marshal Tito and his centralized nationalism. The Croatian National Congress, centered in New York, paid for a large advertisement in The New York Times *on March 14, 1980. The advertisement denounced Tito as a mass murderer and listed "only a few" of his crimes against the Croatian people.*

γ   γ   γ

- In 1945 Tito ordered the massacre of 300,000 Croat soldiers together with many women and children.
- Tito's agents brutally murdered scores of Croat political exiles in Western countries—often unhindered by Western police forces.
- Tito persecuted religions, killing or imprisoning thousands of clergymen, including Cardinal Stepinac, who was kept in confinement until his death in 1960.
- Tito imprisoned and tortured thousands of Croat political prisoners in such terrible prisons as Stara Gradiska, Lepoglava, and Goli Otok.
- Tito's economic policies impoverished and exploited Croatia causing more than a million Croats to leave the country in search of a livelihood.
- In the 1960s Tito encouraged young Croatian idealists to set forth their demands for freedom, but in 1971 reversed himself and imprisoned thousands of intellectuals, students, and workers.

[1]*The New York Times*, March 14, 1980. Copyright © by The New York Times Company. Reprinted by permission.

READING NO. 36

THE TENOR OF BASQUE NATIONALISM[1]

The confrontation between the centralized Spanish regime and Basque nationalism produced spectacular political assassinations, trials, and reprisals. Basque nationalism remains a most powerful opposition movement and is capable of challenging the unity of the Spanish state. Historian Stanley G. Payne presents an account of the ferment to establish an independent Basque country.

γ   γ   γ

During the past decade, however, it has become clear that the dominant political passion of the second half of the twentieth century is nationalism, not any form of social, class, or ideological revolt per se. Nationalism has returned to the center of attention even among totalitarian systems theoretically based on class-conscious internationalism. Regional nationalism among small ethnic groups has gained new momentum all over western Europe.

Modernization, rather than diluting and erasing national consciousness among small ethnic groups, may actually exacerbate it. In the case of Spain, modernization occurred first and most rapidly in regions of distinct identity and local culture, so that the process led to dissociation rather than homogenization. Urbanization sharpened cultural tensions rather than merely transforming them, and the formation of political parties tended to reproduce rather than cut across regional differences. In the Basque country modernization has not even produced the vaunted secularization that is supposedly its inevitable concomitant, and Basque religiosity to a considerable extent has fueled Basque nationalism. The modernization process has led to a

[1]Stanley G. Payne, *Basque Nationalism* (Reno, Nevada, 1975), pp. 249, 251–252. By permission of Stanley G. Payne.

combination of feelings of superiority and exploitation that have undermined the concept of a Spanish nation state. . . .

If the nationalists per se are probably likely to remain a minority within the greater Basque region, they are conversely not likely to fade away or lose their own vigor. With no more than a plurality, nationalism can well reassert itself within a more liberal Spanish system as the leading single factor in the Basque country, resting on the middle classes, the nationalist intelligentsia, and the remaining rural population of Vizcaya and Guipúzcoa. If the opportunity for direct political representation is finally regained, it will not be necessary for nationalism to enroll the bulk of the population in order to regain a broad Basque autonomy. The principle of autonomy is accepted by all the Spanish left and by much of the Spanish center. Nearly all political groups in the Basque region support some form or degree of autonomy. Some form of serious accommodation of regional feeling is virtually assured if anything approaching liberal or democratic government returns to Spain.

Nationalism in the Basque country and Catalonia was born of the contradictions, imbalances, and frustrations in the organization of a modern polity, economy, and culture in Spain. During the past generation these imbalances have been somewhat reduced in the economic sector, but the political and cultural frustrations that gave rise to Basque nationalism remain and are likely to persist for some time to come. The twentieth century bears witness that the spirit and consciousness of small peoples do not easily die.

READING NO. 37

THE FRENCH LANGUAGE AND NATIONALISM IN QUEBEC[1]

René Lévesque, leading Francophone, regarded the French language as the basis of Quebec's nationalism. "At the core of [a distinctive Quebecers personality] is the fact that we speak French. Everything else depends on this one essential element and follows from it or leads back to it." C. Michael MacMillan commented on this blueprint for the Quebec nationalist cause.

γ　　　　　γ　　　　　γ

The link between language and Québec nationalism reveals a thematic continuity for at least this century. A prominent theme is the centrality of the language to the national and cultural identity of French-Canadians. Related to it is the belief that the status and condition of the language are an important barometer of the well-being of the French-Canadian "nation." As one keen student of Québec history remarked, "the state of the French language has always been regarded in Québec as a symptom of the health of the French-Canadian nation." Finally, there is a strong undercurrent of resentment over the dominance of the English language in Québec's social and economic life both for the threat that it poses to the vitality of the French language, and also for its implied slight to the French language in an ostensibly French society. In view of the prominent place language occupies in nationalist thought, the issue ought to figure prominently on the nationalist agenda and also have an impact on the ebb and flow of nationalist sentiment.

---

[1]C. Michael MacMillan, "Language Issues and Nationalism in Quebec." *Canadian Review of Studies in Nationalism*, Vol. XIV, No. 2 (Fall, 1987), p. 232. By permission of the *Canadian Review of Studies in Nationalism*.

READING NO. 38

THE REFERENDUM FOR VOTERS OF QUEBEC, MAY 20, 1980[1]

On May 20, 1980, the voters of Quebec, Canada, were asked to vote on a referendum giving sovereignty to the state of Quebec. The voters were asked to give a simple "Yes" or "No" vote to a problem that had become increasingly irksome. In a large turnout, one of the heaviest in Quebec's history, the French-speaking population rejected the proposal.

γ   γ   γ

The Government of Quebec has made public its proposal to negotiate a new agreement with the rest of Canada, based on the equality of nations.

This agreement would enable Quebec to acquire the exclusive power to make its laws, levy its taxes and establish relations abroad—in other words, sovereignty—and, at the same time, to maintain with Canada an economic association, including a common currency.

No change in political status resulting from these negotiations will be effected without approval by the people through another referendum.

On these terms do you give the Government of Quebec the mandate to negotiate the proposed agreement between Quebec and the rest of Canada?

---

[1] Text of the referendum.

READING NO. 39

CARLTON J. H. HAYES ON NATIONALISM AS A BLESSING OR A CURSE[1]

As early as 1926 Columbia University's Carlton J. H. Hayes, pioneer scholar of nationalism, presented the two sides of nationalism—as a blessing or curse. In his view, nationalism, when combined with the purest patriotism, was a blessing, especially when its precepts and practices of national life do not incite to war or militarism or intolerance. But when nationalism expresses exclusiveness and narrowness, when its propaganda stresses imperialism and war, when it inclines to bare aggression, it develops into a curse for mankind.

γ γ γ

It may appear to some . . . that nationalism is to the human race a curse, and nothing but a curse. On the other hand, it may seem to some critically minded persons that the nationalism hereby cursed is merely a fanciful caricature of a true and real nationalism which to humanity in its present stage of development is not a curse but a blessing.

Regarding the latter point, let us frankly acknowledge that much depends upon the definition of terms. We are fully conscious that despite an earnest effort to speak with precision and to avoid ambiguity we ourselves have been using the word nationalism to indicate two quite different things. We have employed it to denote an actual historical process, the process of establishing nationalities as political units, of building out of tribes and empires the modern institution of the national state. We have also employed the same word to describe a contemporary popular belief, the belief that one's own nationality or

---

[1]Carlton J. H. Hayes, *Essays on Nationalism* (New York, 1926), pp. 245–250. Courtesy of The MacMillan Co.

national state has such intrinsic worth and excellence as to require one to be loyal to it above every other thing and particularly to bestow upon it what amounts to supreme religious worship.

Whether nationalism *as a process* is a curse or a blessing, we have no stomach to declare. We have read enough history to make us timid, if not humble, about passing moral judgment or basing philosophic speculation on great and long continued historic processes. Nationalism as an historic process has been great and long continued, and to regret and condemn it would be for us purely academic diversions; we couldn't undo it if we would; we certainly couldn't refashion all those multitudinous factors, personal and social, economic and political, religious and cultural, which during many centuries now past recall have transformed city-states and imperial states into national states. Nationalism of this sort is not a proper subject of praise or blame; it is simply a fact, and a fact as little deserving of benediction or anathema as the fact that man has two legs or the fact that the earth revolves about the sun.

But nationalism as a belief belongs to another category. To every thoughtful person, save only the unqualified fatalist, it is as fitting to criticise nationalism of this kind as to criticise any other popular creed, say Christianity or Socialism or Liberalism; it is important for our generation and for that which follows us that we should judge all living growing trees by their fruit, and that if to our taste any tree brings forth evil fruit we should attempt to cut down or at least engraft good fruit upon that tree. It is nationalism as a popular contemporary belief concerning which we would put the question, is it curse or is it blessing? And, reverting to the first sentence of this essay, we would unhesitatingly affirm that, judged by its fruitage of intolerance, militarism, and war, nationalism as the belief which we have indicated is evil and should be cursed—and cured.

It is possible, of course, to use the word nationalism, as some writers have used it, to indicate "wholesome national patriotism" and to describe certain precepts and practices of national life which do not incite to war or militarism or intolerance. But let us not dodge the issue by verbal quibbling. Grant that there is a rampant, blatant nationalism which produces evil fruitage and which is a curse, and it will gladly be conceded that there may be a sweet amiable nationalism which will bring forth good fruit in abundance and will be to all men a solace and a blessing. . . .

. . . It has been a prime purpose of the present study to demonstrate that nationalism is a complex of nationality, national state, and national patriotism. To our way of thinking, none of these elements in itself is moral or immoral, good or bad; each may be put to good use and each is liable to abuse. What basically gives one or another—perhaps all three— an evil appearance today is their intimate association in a new trinity and unity of nationalism. Failure to recognize this fact is probably the most plausible explanation of the differences among recent critics and students of the subject. Nationalism— the combination of nationality, the national state, and national patriotism, as effected in our age—is the indivisible source of grave abuses and evils.

What, in summary, are these grave evils and abuses? First is the spirit of exclusiveness and narrowness. The national state, through education in national school, national army, and national journalism, through the social pressure of national patriotism, inculcates in its citizens the fancy that they are a world by themselves, sufficient unto themselves; it teaches them that they are a chosen people, a peculiar people, and that they should prize far more what is theirs as a nationality than what is theirs as human beings. It is this spirit of exclusiveness and narrowness which thrives on, and in turn nurses, a smugness that is laughable, an ignorance that is dangerous, and an uncritical pride that can be reduced, if at all, only by a beating.

Secondly, nationalism places a premium on uniformity. It prescribes national models of art, national standards of thought, and national norms of conduct, and to these it expects all the inhabitants of each national state to conform. Individual differences, class differences, religious differences, are alike deemed unfortunate; and the individual of genius is suspect, especially if his genius displays itself in criticism of national uniformity. If nationality does something to prevent the reduction of the whole world to a drab sameness, then nationalism does much more within a nationality to overlay local colour with its own dull greyness.

Thirdly, nationalism increases the docility of the masses. As a result of their national upbringing and their life-long nationalist education, they are seldom inclined to question the providential character of their nationality, of their state, of their government, or of the economic circumstances in which they live. If only a leader appeals to them in the cause of national patriotism, they are prepared to follow that leader unquestioningly and unhesitatingly into any undertaking upon which he has set his heart. In the name of national rights, national interest, and national honour, they will forego their own individual rights, sacrifice their own individual interests, and even forswear their own individual honour. They are ready in the name of the liberty and freedom of their nationality to abridge the liberty of fellow citizens and to take away the freedom of other nationalities. They have, in supreme degree, the will to believe, and this will to believe renders them easy dupes of nationalist propaganda in support of imperialism and war.

Fourthly, nationalism in its present form focuses popular attention upon war and preparedness for war. War is that historic tradition of a nationality which the national state, under present conditions, does most to keep alive and active in the minds and hearts of its citizens. Military heroes outrank in national pantheons the heroes of science and art and learning. Baseball or cricket or mahjong may be a national game of a particular people, but of all nationalists the world over the biggest and best sport is national fighting. But the more the people train for the great sport of fighting, the more they deify their soldiers, and the more they cherish the memory of the prowess of their ancestors, the less disposed will they be to give time or thought to social reform and preparedness for enduring peace. It is notorious how quickly a popular interest in some educational or economic problem evaporates when confronted by the fierce heat of nationalist passion for military "defense."

From the foregoing general evils and abuses of nationalism proceeds the impulse toward those specific abuses and evils which have been discussed at length in earlier essays— intolerance, militarism, and war. Or, if one likes, one may reorganize the material in those essays and deduce from it, as the fifth, sixth, and seventh outstanding evils of nationalism, respectively Jingoism, Imperialism, Intolerance.

An intolerant attitude and behaviour towards one's fellows; a belief in the imperial mission of one's own nationality at the expense of others, particularly at the expense of backward peoples; a habit of carrying a chip on one's national shoulder and defying another nationality to knock it off; a fond dwelling on the memory of past wars and a feverish preparing for future wars, to the neglect of present civil problems; a willingness to be led and guided by self-styled patriots; a diffidence, almost a panic, about thinking or acting differently from one's fellows; a spirit of exclusiveness and narrowness which feeds on gross ignorance of others and on inordinate pride in one's self and one's nationality: these are all too prevalent aspects of contemporary nationalism. If in these respects nationalism is not mitigated it will be an unqualified curse to future generations.

BOYD C. SHAFER ON THE "BLESSINGS" OF NATIONALISM[1]

Outstanding scholar of nationalism Boyd C. Shafer commented on Carlton J. H. Hayes's description of the "blessings and curses" of nationalism. In discussing its "blessings," Shafer emphasized the reasons for the staying power of this historical phenomenon.

γ   γ   γ

Nationalism has, nonetheless, brought much that has been labelled "curse" or "blessing." Here the "blessings" can be but too briefly noted. The building of nations and national sentiment in Europe and later all parts of the world brought reduction of hampering provincial guild, and feudal restrictions on trade and production thus allowing those enlargements of markets and the division of labor that increased production and wealth as *both* the fathers of capitalism and communism, Adam Smith and Karl Marx, believed. And differing nationalities as the Russian dissident novelist Alexander Solzhenitsyn so vehemently asserted, may bring diversities of life styles, "special colors" to brighten the dullness of uniformity. Of course it is individuals who give diversity to life but Solzhenitsyn and others also think in terms of nations.

For individuals within established or becoming nations, nationalism gave joy in service and in "doing one's duty." It also provided excitement in competition with other nationalities as well as in domestic ceremonies and celebrations, not only for the privileged few but also for working men who Karl Marx declared in 1848 had "no country." Nationalism brought hope

---

[1]Boyd C. Shafer, *Nationalism and Internationalism: Belonging in Human Experience* (Malabar, Fla., 1982), pp. 112–113. By permission of Boyd C. Shafer.

(however illusory) for a better, fuller, freer life for a safer order and more just justice; it gave patriots even ordinary people opportunity to feel glory, splendor, pride; it united them in feeling against potential and actual national enemies, while it lowered tensions among individuals and groups within nations by motivating work and production, and by allowing them to vent frustrations and angers against "outsiders." The "feeling of belonging" as a recent student of war, Stanislaw Andreski, put it, "to a group, which appears to be indispensable to human happiness, does require some measure of antagonism to other groups"—hostilization.

Above all, perhaps, nationalism provided people traditions, roots, refuges in times of trouble, and enlarged family home, therefore an identity which other people recognized even if they did not always respect. In times of joy or despair, in the words of a distinguished anthropologist-psychologist Lévi-Strauss, it enabled them to avoid "the one real calamity, the one fatal flaw" (afflicting "groups of men that prevents their fulfillment"— "*aloneness*" (*author's ital.*).

That national blessings sometimes turn out to be illusions makes little difference. People believed. But that group solidarities did bring opposing solidarities did make a difference as the Russians found out in dealing with the nationalisms of Central and Eastern Europe, with the Polish trade union Solidarity (1980), for example.

READING NO. 41

BARBARA WARD ON THE
STAYING POWER OF NATIONALISM[1]

Barbara Ward, able British journalist, saw nationalism as the most powerful dissolvent of empires the world has ever known. She attributed its staying power as the manifestation of the Western search for freedom under law and as the organizing principle of human society.

γ   γ   γ

IN APPROACHING the problems of our modern world we should, I think, try to begin where the real center of power lies. I hardly need to insist that underlying most issues in national and international relations is the problem of power: power in the simplest sense of men being able ultimately to make other people do what they want. In our world, this final power is exercised by the state: under a despotic government by force, under a democratic government largely by consent; but in the last analysis any kind of government rests on its ability to impose its policies and to achieve its will. This is the absolute sovereignty exercised by the state alone.

The state is thus the nodal point of all our problems. Since we are concerned with world affairs, the aspect of the state which we have to study is largely its relations with other states. This is the field in which lie the tensions, the possibilities, the whole vista of international politics. But it might be as well to begin by looking at the state itself in isolation. We imagine we know what we mean when we talk of the state; yet it is a concept that has changed out of all recognition over the centuries. What we think about it today is not at all what our ancestors thought of it. . . .

[1]Barbara Ward, *Five Ideas That Change the World* (New York, 1959), pp. 13–14, 28, 33. Courtesy of W. W. Norton Co., Inc.

At the moment I would say that, looking around our modern world with its changing institutions, its social and economic developments, and its new forms of growth, we are perfectly justified in saying that nationalism is by far the strongest political force with which we have to reckon. . . .

Nationalism in this sense is a manifestation of the Western search for freedom under law as *the* organizing principle of human society. As such, it is the most powerful dissolvent of empires the world has ever known. And I am not thinking only of the energy it gives to those who seek to be free. I am thinking, too, of its effect upon the governors.

READING NO. 42

BARBARA WARD ON THE TEMPORARY DIMINUTION OF NATIONALISM[1]

British journalist Barbara Ward judged that after World War II the feeling was widespread that nationalism as the most violent force in world society, was to some extent in retreat. But the consciousness of nationalism soon returned as a dangerous force in world society.

γ　　　　　γ　　　　　γ

For ten or fifteen years after the war, the feeling in the Western world that nationalism was no longer the dominant political philosophy was fairly strong and secure. But now we are beginning to realize that nationalism has a lot of life in it still. The feelings in which nationalism is rooted and to which it can appeal are by no means dead. A revived Western Europe, a decline in Soviet belligerency, Chinese resurgence—all these changes in the world balance of power have changed emotions and reactions too. We may not yet know how general this revival is. Nor do we know whether it reaches out to a new generation. But we do know that some voices are now raised to talk once again in terms of absolute loyalty to the primacy of the nation-state.

[1] Barbara Ward, *Nationalism and Ideology* (New York, 1966), pp. 12–13. Courtesy of W. W. Norton Co., Inc.

READING NO. 43

ELIE KEDOURIE ON THE DANGEROUS RESULTS OF NATIONALISM[1]

The British scholar, Elie Kedourie, deeply interested in the phenomenon of nationalism, points out that the power of an ongoing nationalism does not necessarily make for greater peace and stability. In his view the system of nation-states was not necessarily an improvement in political life.

γ   γ   γ

The attempts to refashion so much of the world on national lines has not led to greater peace and stability. On the contrary, it has created new conflicts, exacerbated tensions, and brought catastrophe to numberless people innocent of all politics. The history of Europe since 1919, in particular, has shown the disastrous possibilities inherent in nationalism. In the mixed area of Central and Eastern Europe, and the Balkans, empires disappeared, their ruling groups were humbled and made to pay, for a time, the penalty of previous arrogance. Whether these empires were doomed anyway, or whether it would have been possible to preserve them is mere speculation. What can be said with certainty is that the nation-states who inherited the position of the empires were not an improvement. They did not minister to political freedom, they did not increase prosperity, and their existence was not conducive to peace; in fact, the national question which their setting up, it was hoped, would solve, became, on the contrary, more bitter and envenomed: it was a national question, that of the German minorities in the new nation-states, which occasioned the outbreak of the Second

[1]Elie Kedourie, *Nationalism* (New York, 1960), pp. 138–139. By permission of Elie Kedourie.

World War. What may be said of Europe can with equal justice be said of the Middle East, or of South-East Asia, wherever the pressure of circumstances or the improvidence of rulers or their failure of nerve made possible the triumph of nationalist programmes. The verdict of Lord Acton rendered in the middle of the last century would seem to be prophetic, temperate and just: '. . . nationality,' he wrote, 'does not aim either at liberty or prosperity, both of which it sacrifices to the imperative necessity of making the nation the mould and measure of the State. Its course will be marked with material as well as moral ruin, in order that a new invention may prevail over the works of God and the interests of mankind.' The invention has prevailed, and the best that can be said for it is that it is an attempt to establish once and for all the reign of justice in a corrupt world, and to repair, for ever, the injuries of time. But this best is bad enough, since to repair such injuries other injuries must in turn be inflicted, and no balance is ever struck in the grisly account of cruelty and violence. For we do know with certainty that no government lasts for ever, that one government goes and another comes to take its place, and that the ways of Providence are inscrutable. To welcome a change or to regret it, because one set of rulers has gone and another has come, is something which we all do, for some rulers are more likely to look to our own welfare than others; but these are private preoccupations for which such private justification is reasonable. Public justification requires more; to welcome or deplore a change in government because some now enjoy power and others are deprived of it is not enough. The only criterion capable of public defence is whether the new rulers are less corrupt and grasping, or more just and merciful, or whether there is no change at all, but the corruption, the greed, and the tyranny merely find victims other than those of the departed rulers. And this is really the only question at issue between nationalism and the systems to which it is opposed. It is a question which, in the nature of the case, admits of no final and conclusive answer.

READING NO. 44

SHAPING OF THE "NEW EUROPE"[1]

On November 19–21, 1990, twenty-four member nations attended a Conference on Security and Cooperation in Europe (C.S.C.E.) to discuss the status of "the New Europe." The authorities in reunited Germany expressed strong approval of European unity.

γ γ γ

The Conference on Security and Cooperation in Europe (CSCE) took place from Monday through Wednesday (November 19–21) in Paris, with all 34 member nations attending.

Immediately before the conference began on Monday, the 16 member nations of NATO and the six Warsaw Pact nations signed a far-reaching disarmament accord, the "Declaration of Twenty-two." According to the terms of the agreement, neither side may have more than 20,000 tanks, 30,000 armored vehicles, 20,000 artillery pieces, 6,800 combat aircraft, and 2,000 helicopters. Germany also agreed to set a 370,000 person limit on troops.

The conference culminated in the signing of the 20-page "Paris Charter for a New Europe—A New Age of Democracy" on Wednesday. The document declares bindingly that democracy is the "only form of government" and says that this "cannot be reversed." In the area of security policy, the document provides for the continuation of the Vienna negotiations on conventional forces and says that the negotiations should be completed by 1992. The document also calls for increased cooperation in security matters and for economic support of countries that are "on the path to a free market economy." Another important provision is the establishment of the first

---

[1]German Information Center, *The Week in Germany*. November 23, 1990, p. 1. Courtesy of *This Week in Germany*.

CSCE organizations, including a center for conflict resolution, which is to be temporarily established in Vienna; after the next summit in Helsinki in 1992, it may be moved there. A secretariat for the CSCE is to be established in Prague. There will be a schedule for meetings, including biannual summits and annual foreign minister meetings. German unity is praised in the charter as "a significant contribution to a lasting, just, peaceful order in a united and democratic Europe."

Chancellor Kohl called the charter the "Magna Carta of freedom." He expressed willingness to aid eastern European countries and expressed thanks for the international support for German unity. "In consciousness of German history and the moral and political responsibility it places upon us, Germany will strive to be a cornerstone in the peaceful European order," he said. President Bush stated, "We have closed a chapter in history . . . the Cold War is over."

READING NO. 45

BREAKUP OF YUGOSLAVIA PROPHESIED[1]

Observers of the Yugoslav scene were convinced that the clash of ethnic groups would lead eventually to the dissolution of the nation-state. The compounding nationalism and the concomitant worsening of ethnic relations led to predictions that the country could no longer remain a viable nation-state.

γ　　　　γ　　　　γ

WASHINGTON, Nov. 27—United States intelligence is predicting that federated Yugoslavia will break apart, most probably in the next 18 months, and that civil war in that multinational Balkan country is highly likely.

The predictions, included in a long National Intelligence Estimate produced under the auspices of the Central Intelligence Agency, are unusually firm and sharp for such a document, a senior Government official said.

The intelligence estimate runs counter to views of Yugoslavia's future in the State Department, although some specialists in that department also subscribe to the premise.

The intelligence prediction received backing in Yugoslavia on Nov. 15 when Prime Minister Ante Markovic declared: "The acts of the highest state organs of Slovenia, Serbia and, partly, Croatia inevitably lead to a straining of political relations in Yugoslavia and directly threaten the country's survival."

Nationalism Is Growing. The Prime Minister continued, "The situation is characterized by growing nationalism and separatism and an alarming worsening of ethnic relations, all of which is expressed in violence, a drastic threat to public order, peace and citizens' safety."

---

[1]*The New York Times*, November 28, 1990. Copyright © by The New York Times Company. Reprinted by permission.

According to United States officials who have read the intelligence document, its two basic findings are that "the Yugoslav experiment has failed, that the country will break up" and that "this is likely to be accompanied by ethnic violence and unrest which could lead to civil war."

"It did not predict absolutely that there would be a civil war, but said it was highly likely," one official noted. He said he was "startled by its stark terms."

READING NO. 46

JULIUS BRAUNTHAL ON
THE PARADOX OF NATIONALISM[1]

*Carlton J. H. Hayes's formula of nationalism as blessing or
curse has retained its popularity to the present day. In this
excerpt Julius Braunthal, a British writer and critic, repeated
the moral paradox of nationalism.*

γ   γ   γ

What is the essence of the sentiment of nationalism—this
sentiment which appears to override every other human sentiment, and to prompt men to sacrifice everything to its idol?

It is, in the first place, a noble sentiment, because it embodies
attachment to a cause wider than that of one's self and one's
family. It is also a noble sentiment because it embodies the pride
of the cultural achievement of one's own nation. It is further a
natural sentiment, because it embodies everyone's love for the
plot of earth on which one was born. So everyone is swayed with
the same emotion for his own country as W. E. Henley was when
he, expressing it for the English, wrote the lines:

> Life is good and joy runs high
> Between English earth and sky.

Yet nationalism embodies more than merely the natural and
universal sentiment of devotion to one's own kin, language,
culture and plot of land. By identification of nation and state,
nationalism is the expression of an absolute, exclusive devotion
to one's country. It refuses to recognise the common bond of
humanity; it is the antithesis to the Christian concept of the
brotherhood of all men; it is the sentiment of extended selfish-
ness which sets the nation above every moral law. Every nationalism is guided by the principle: "My country, right or wrong."

---

[1]Julius Braunthal, *The Paradox of Nationalism* (London, 1946), pp. 29–30.
Courtesy of St. Bodolph Publishing Co., London.

READING NO. 47

LATIN AMERICAN NATIONALISM AND A CRITIQUE OF YANKEEISM[1]

When on a 1958 good-will tour in Latin America, Vice President Richard M. Nixon was spat upon by young demonstrators in Venezuela. After the incident, José Figueres, former President of Costa Rica, appeared before a Congressional Committee and issued a blunt statement to the American people revealing why Mr. Nixon had been received in so unfriendly a fashion. His explanation of why even spitting was deserved reveals the emotion behind Latin-American nationalism. "People cannot spit at a foreign policy. . . . Their only remaining recourse is to spit."

γ   γ   γ

As a citizen of the Hemisphere, as a man who has dedicated his public life to the cultivation of inter-American understanding, as a student who knows and esteems the United States, and who has never tried to conceal that esteem from anyone, no mater how hostile, I deplore the fact that the people of Latin America, as represented by a handful of over-excited Venezuelans, should have spat at a worthy functionary, who represents the greatest nation of our times. But I must speak frankly, even rudely, because I believe that the situation requires it: people cannot spit at a foreign policy, which is what they wanted to do. And when they have run out of other ways of making themselves understood, their only remaining recourse is to spit.

With all due respect for Vice President Nixon, and with all my admiration for his conduct, which was, during the events, heroic, and afterwards, noble, I must explain that the act of

[1]José Figueres, in *Hearings Before the Subcommittee on Inter-American Affairs of the Committee on Foreign Relations, Second Session* (Washington, D.C., 1958), extracted from pp. 71–93. Courtesy of U.S. Government Printing Office.

spitting, vulgar though it is, is without substitute in our language for expressing certain emotions. . . .

If you are going to talk about human dignity to Russia, why is it so difficult to talk about the dignity of man to the Dominican Republic? Which is intervention, which nonintervention? Is it that a mere potential menace to your own liberties is, essentially, more serious than the consummated rape of our liberties?

Of course, you have made certain investments in the American dictatorships. The aluminum companies extract bauxite almost gratis. Your generals, your admirals, your civil functionaries, and your magnates receive royal treatment there. As your Senate verified yesterday, some concessionaires bribe the reigning dynasties with millions for the privilege of hunting on their grounds. They deduct the money from the taxes they pay in the United States, but it returns to the country, and upon arrival in Hollywood is converted into extravagant furs and automobiles which shatter the fragile virtue of the female stars.

Meanwhile, our women are raped by gangsters, our men castrated in the torture chambers, and our illustrious professors disappear lugubriously from the halls of Columbia University in New York. When one of your legislators calls this "collaboration to combat communism," 180 million Latin Americans want to spit.

Spitting is a despicable practice, when it is physically performed. But what about moral spitting? When your government invited Pedro Estrada, the Himmler of the Western Hemisphere, to be honored in Washington, did you not spit in the faces of all the democrats of America?

. . . I can assure you that, in international economic policy, the United States gives the appearance of being bent on repeating certain errors of the domestic policy which did so much damage in the past, not excepting, of course, those which led to the great crisis in 1929.

We Latin Americans are tired of pointing out these mistakes, especially the lack of interest in the prices of our products. Every time we suggest some plan to stabilize prices at a just level, you answer us with slogans, with such novelties as "the law of supply and demand," or "the system of free interprise," or with insults as "Aren't we giving you enough money now?"

We are not asking for hand-outs, except in cases of emergency. We are not people who would spit for money. We have inherited all the defects of the Spanish character, but also some of its virtues. Our poverty does not abate our pride. We have our dignity.

What we want is to be paid a just price for the sweat of our people, the sap of our soil, when we supply some needed product to another country. This would be enough for us to live, and to raise our own capital, and to pursue our own development.

READING NO. 48

JOHN BOWLE ON
THE FUTURE OF NATIONALISM[1]

Among those who saw nationalism as a phase in modern historical development was John Bowle, Professor of Political Theory at the College of Europe in Bruges, Belgium. According to Bowle, national freedom can only be obtained by a voluntary pooling of sovereignties in a regional, and ultimately a world context. In his view, although nationalism still persists, it is likely to prove only a phase of historical development.

γ   γ   γ

Nationalism will . . . either reinforce world order or be exploited by the doctrinaire of class war. Its destiny will be determined through institutions and ideas. In spite of great dangers, the institutional prospect is not altogether discouraging. The machinery of international conciliation exists. U.N.O. at least provides a setting in which national and class conflicts can be debated before a world audience. As popular understanding of the appalling consequences of modern war sinks in, this audience may draw its own conclusions; even, perhaps, make itself felt. And if modern public diplomacy shocks diplomats of the old school, it is at least preferable to war. The cosmopolitan influence of U.N.O.'s subsidiary agencies is also likely to increase. The project of by-passing destructive nationalism and class war by a common exploitation of nuclear power is at least on the agenda.

The United Nations can provide the rallying point for liberal nationalism and develop with the grain of nationalist sentiment, not against it. It must adapt and sublimate the nationalist idea, to attempt its eradication.

---

[1]John Bowle, *The Nationalist Idea* (London, 1955), pp. 61–64. Courtesy of Ampersand Ltd.

Such a policy demands self-discipline, even sacrifice. The Western peoples and their allies refrain from conflict within their own boundaries, but they still present a singular exclusiveness to the outer world, in particular when "their standards of living" are imperilled. Can the peoples, or even their responsible rulers, be brought to the point of sacrificing national interests, even within the British Commonwealth or a European community, let alone lower their economic standards to mitigate the enormous poverty of Africa and the East? Is not economic nationalism so deeply engrained as to obstruct even the day-to-day working of the present system, and certainly to prevent it being changed? The movement of industry, the temporary unemployment and displacement, implied by any economic rationalisation of Europe has already aroused not merely the hostility of politicians, but popular resentment. The facts of world strategy and economy are now supra-national. But will popular nationalism accept them, save under compulsion?

These deep-rooted prejudices, inherited from the nineteenth century, can be transcended only by a new interpretation of nationalism. It would accept the fact that national freedom can only be secured by a voluntary pooling of sovereignties, in a regional, and ultimately a world, context. This version of liberal nationalism would be only an adaptation of the original Mazzinian ideal of the "sisterhood" of nations. Such a development is not necessarily impossible. History does not stand still. Just as the nineteenth-century nation state promoted a political outlook that was new, so modern political developments are likely to promote a political theory suited to our own time. This sublimation and adaptation of nationalism may even be swift. Modern mass communications, properly handled, could greatly accelerate it. The rise of popular nationalism, if it can be diverted from destructive aims, may then, after all, prove an advance. If a society becomes a nation when it thinks it is one, a supranational consciousness can arise in the same way, particularly when promoted by the trend of economic and technological change and the menace of tyrannical aggression.

For the lesson of the history of nationalism is surely this. That the sovereign nationalism of the nineteenth century, though it still persists, is likely to prove only a phase of political development. It is comparatively recent in the total panorama of history;

it may give place to the wider outlook. If it does not link liberal nationalism to world institutions which will secure the rule of law, it will be crushed by the totalitarians. This challenge may unite more and more free people against it. All ideologies shift and change, and all societies develop. We may yet witness the development of the nationalist idea into a world view, in spite of the frightful catastrophes its debasement may still bring about.

READING NO. 49

FLORA LEWIS ON THE TIDES OF HISTORY[1]

In one of her columns for the op-ed page of The New York Times, *Flora Lewis, commenting on "tides of history," wrote about the current surge in nationalism. She also sees a developing interest in cooperation among peoples. She believes that the tide of history is moving slowly against the old instincts, but it is moving because of a new understanding that no part of the world can be truly isolated.*

γ   γ   γ

The village, the tribe, the nation arose as protective associations throughout the story of civilization. They organized against the outsider and command fierce loyalties, so much that they provide a definition of identity.

They create a community of language, of culture, of belief, of the dignity that every human seeks. No wonder that when alien rule can successfully be challenged, there is a tremendous urge to independence, to deliberately stress distinctions between "us" and "them." Nationalism is on the rise wherever rule was imposed from outside.

But this renewed surge of nationalism comes at a time when independence can be seen more as an illusion. People are inescapably at the mercy of their neighbors if they are not to live as hermits, and all are becoming neighbors. The question is only whether force or consent and cooperation will dominate their relations.

That lay behind the ideas of Jean Monnet when he conceived of what has become the European Community, as his Dutch associate Max Kohnstamm recently pointed out. The economy

---

of size, the mutual benefit of opening markets and reliable institutions created the incentives to pool jealously cherished bits of sovereignty, step by step.

"What gives me so much hope is that the Community shows it is possible to change structures that enclose nations in seemingly unbreakable vicious circles," Mr. Kohnstamm said. Monnet's purpose was to launch a "process of change that would bring a new structure of international relations, protected and constrained by laws uniting people in common responsibilities."

That tide is only beginning to rise, but it too is part of change in our time. In fits and starts, the world is going that way because it has to. Whether they make dramatic headlines or are barely discernible, the impulses of history are moving.

BIBLIOGRAPHY

Aksin, Bangamin, *States and Nations* (London, 1964).

Armstrong, J. H., *Ukrainian Nationalism* (New York, 1963).

Azrael, Jeremy R. (ed.), *Soviet Nationality: Politics and Practices* (New York, 1981).

Barclay, Glen St. J., *Twentieth Century Nationalism: Revolution* (New York, 1972).

Barghoorn, Frederick, C., *Soviet Russian Nationalism* (New York, 1956).

Barker, Ernest, *National Character and the Factors in Its Formation* (New York and London, 1927).

Bell, Wendell and Walter E. Freeman (eds.), *Ethnicity and Nation-Building* (Beverly Hills, CA, 1974).

Berlin, Isaiah, "The Bent Twig: A Note on Nationalism," *Foreign Affairs*, LI, No. 1 (October, 1972), 11–30.

Birch, A. H., "Minority Nationalist Movements and Theories of Political Integration," *World Politics*, XXX, No. 3 (April, 1978), 325–345.

Bossenbrook, W., *Mid-Twentieth Century Nationalism* (Detroit, 1965).

Chadwick, H. M. *The Nationalities of Europe and the Growth of National Ideologies* (Cambridge, England, 1945).

Cobban, Alfred, *The Nation-State and National Self-Determination* (rev. ed., London, 1969).

Connor, Walker, "Self-Determination: The New Phase," *World Politics*, XX, No. 1 (October, 1967), 30–53.

————. "The Politics of Ethnonationalism," *Journal of International Affairs*, XXVII, No. 1 (1973), 1–21.

————. "Nationalism and Political Illegitimacy," *Canadian Review of Studies in Nationalism*, VIII, No. 2 (Fall, 1981), 201–222.

Coudenhove-Kalergi, Richard N., *Europa Erwacht* (*Europe Awakens*), (Paris, 1934).

————. *Crusade for Pan-Europe* (New York, 1943).

————. *Pan-Europa* (Munich, 1966).

Deutsch, Karl W., *Nationalism and Social Communication: An*

Inquiry into the Foundations of Nationality (2nd ed., Cambridge, Mass., 1966).

Doob, Leonard, W., *Patriotism and Nationalism: Their Psychological Foundations* (New Haven, Ct., 1964).

Duijker, H. C. and N. H. Frijjda, *National Character and National Stereotypes* (Amsterdam, Holland, 1960).

Emerson, Rupert, *From Empire to Nation: The Rise of Self-Assertion of Asian and African Peoples* (Cambridge, Mass., 1960).

Ergang, Robert R., *Herder and the Foundations of German Nationalism* (New York, 1931).

Fishman, Joshua, *Language and Nationality* (Rowley, Mass., 1972).

Forbes, H. D., "Two Approaches to the Psychology of Nationalism," *Canadian Review of Studies in Nationalism*, II, No. 1. (Fall, 1974), 172–181.

Fyfe, Hamilton, *The Illusion of National Character* (London, 1940).

Glaser, Nathan and Daniel P. Moynihan, *Ethnicity: Theory and Experience* (Cambridge, Mass., 1975).

Gordon, D. C., *Self-Determination and History in the Third World* (Princeton, N. J., 1971).

Handley, Richard N., *Nationalism and the Politics of Culture in Quebec* (Madison, Wisc., 1988).

Hayes, Carlton, J. H., *Essays on Nationalism* (New York, 1926).
———. France, *A Nation of Patriots* (New York, 1930).
———. *Nationalism: A Religion* (New York, 1930).

Hertz, Friedrich, *Nationality in History and Politics: A Study of the Psychology and Sociology of National Sentiment and Character* (London, 1944).

Hoover, Arlie J., *The Gospel of Nationalism* (Stuttgart, 1983).

Kann, Robert A., *The Multinational Empire: Nationalism and Reform in the Hapsburg Monarchy, 1848–1918* (2 vols., New York, 1956, 1964).

Kedourie, Elie, *Nationalism* (London and New York, 1966).

Klineberg, Otto, "A Science of National Character," *Journal of Social Psychology* (XIX (1944), 147–162).

Kohn, Hans, *The Idea of Nationalism: A Study of Its Origin and Background* (New York, 1944, 1966).

————. "The Era of German Nationalism," *Journal of the History of Ideas*, XII (1951), 256–274).

————. *Nationalism: Its Meaning and History* (Princeton, N. J., 1956).

McNeill, William H., *Polyethnicity and National Unity in World Politics* (Toronto, 1986).

Namier, Lewis, *Vanished Supremacies: Essays on European History* (London, 1958).

Newman, Gerald, *The Rise of English Nationalism: A Cultural History 1740–1830* (New York, 1987).

O'Brien, Connor Cruise, *God Land, Reflections on Religion and Nationalism* (Cambridge, Mass. and London, 1988).

Payne, Stanley, G., *Basque Nationalism* (Reno, Nev., 1973).

Platt, W., *National Character in Action* (New Brunswick, N. J., 1971).

Ramet, Pedro, *Nationalism and Federalism in Yugoslavia, 1963–1983* (Bloomington, Ind., 1985).

Ronan, Dov, *The Quest for Self-Determination* (New York and London, 1979).

Seton-Watson, Hugh, *Nation and States* (London, 1977).

Shafer, Boyd C., *Nationalism: Myth and Reality* (New York, 1955).

————. *Faces of Nationalism: New Realities and Old Myths* (New York, 1972).

————. *Nationalism and Internationalism: Belonging in Human Experience* (Malabar, Fla., 1982).

Silvert, K. H., *Expectant Peoples: Nationalism and Development* (New York, 1963).

Smith, Anthony D., *Theories of Nationalism* (London, 1971).

————. *Nationalist Movements* (London, 1976).

Snyder, Louis L. (ed.), *The Dynamics of Nationalism* (Princeton, N.J., 1964).

————. *Global Mini-Nationalisms: Autonomy or Independence* (Westport, CT., 1982).

————. *Encyclopedia of Nationalism* (New York, 1990).

Sugar, Peter and Ivo Lederer, *Nationalism in Eastern Europe* (Seattle, 1979).

Symmons-Symonolewicz, K., *Nationalist Movements: A Comparative Analysis* (Meadville, Pa., 1970).

Rudjman, F., *Nationalism in Contemporary Europe* (Boulder, Colo., 1981).

Ward, Barbara, *Nationalism and Ideology* (New York, 1966).

Znaniecki, Florian, *Modern Nationalities: A Sociological Study* (Urbana, Ill., 1952).

INDEX